INTRODUCTION

The healthy recipes for children in this book have been divided into many sections including breakfast, school meals, afternoon tea, dinner, side dishes, desserts, party food and many more.

The recipes are healthy because they have a high nutritional content without sacrificing flavour.

Children have no instinctive sense of what foods are nutritious and therefore need to be taught by parents and teachers. Tell them about good nutrition. They love to know what food does for them. Involve your children in the preparation of meals.

Children will develop healthy eating habits most effectively by following the example set by parents. To promote this, eat together as a family as often as possible.

Avoid buying sweet biscuits, soft drinks, cordials, chips and other "empty energy" (non-nutritious) foods regularly. Better habits will develop if these foods are not kept or seen at home. Children will tend to get into the habit of eating fruit at home if it is available, especially if they see their parents eating it.

Encourage lots of physical activity to build up healthy appetites and help prevent obesity. Serve regular meals — breakfasts, lunch or packed lunches for school and dinner. Give them small servings and allow them to ask for more.

The best way to treat children's refusal of food is to ignore it. Allow them to wait until the next meal so they can build up an appetite again. If "problem eaters" develop give them an empty plate and allow them to serve themselves from serving dishes at the table. If they choose nothing make no comment.

Never bribe, threat, punish or praise with food or force them to eat. Healthy food is something children need and as parents we should provide. Snacks need to be small and nutritious to keep them going between meals without taking away their appetite for the next meal.

It is best not to be fanatical about healthy food. Children will come into contact with unhealthy food at parties and other people's houses. That's fine so long as most of their food is healthy.

Healthy eating habits are easier to establish for our children if we use a wide variety from the five food groups. (See page 48.)

Editor Philip Gore **Art Director** Craig Osment **Art Production** Stephen Joseph **Cookery Editor** Loukie Werle **Food Stylist** Wendy Berecry **Recipes** Lucy Kelly **Photography** Warren Webb **Assistant** Belinda Warn **Typesetting** APT **Printed** in Japan by Dai Nippon Tokyo **Published** by Century Publishing Pty Ltd, 216-224 Commonwealth Street, Surry Hills, NSW 2010 Australia. **UK Distribution** T.B. Clarke (UK) Distributors Ltd, Beckett House, 14 Billing Road, Northampton NN1 5AW. Phone: (0604) 230941 Fax: (0604) 230942. **Australian Distribution** (Supermarkets) Select Magazines Pty Ltd, Suite 402, 7 Merriwa Street, Gordon, NSW 2072. (Newsagents) NDD, 150 Bourke Road, Alexandria, NSW 2015. ©Century Publishing Pty Ltd. *Recommended retail price. **Photography credits:** We gratefully acknowledge **The Design Store,** Spit Junction; **Barbara's House & Garden,** Birkenhead Point; **Opus,** Paddington; **Made Where,** Double Bay; **Australian East India Company,** Bondi Junction; **Hale Imports,** Brookvale; **Casa Shopping,** Darlinghurst; **Pazotti Tiles,** Woollahra; **Country Floors,** Woollahra.

START THE DAY RIGHT

There's no more important meal in your children's day. Breakfast should be nourishing and appetising and needn't be boringly predictable.

Tomato Cheese Puffs

2 tomatoes, sliced
1 small onion
15g (½oz) butter
1 cup grated cheese
4 eggs, beaten
100g (3½oz) natural yoghurt
1 tblspn chopped parsley

1 Place one slice of tomato in the base of four, one cup capacity ovenproof dishes.

2 Saute onion in butter until tender, divide evenly into tomato-lined dishes. Sprinkle evenly with half the cheese.

3 Beat eggs and yoghurt together, pour into dishes. Top each dish with a slice of tomato.

4 Sprinkle with remaining cheese and parsley. Stand on oven tray, bake in moderate oven 30 minutes. Turn out immediately, invert into serving plates.

Serves 4

Chicken Sausage Sticks

Make these sausage sticks on the weekend for a tasty change.

4 long, thin chicken sausages
½ punnet cherry tomatoes, halved
125g (4oz) baby mushrooms
2 tblspn sweet chutney

1 Cut sausages into 2cm (¾in) pieces.

2 Thread sausage pieces onto skewers alternately with cherry tomato halves and baby mushrooms. Brush with chutney.

3 Cook skewers under hot grill both sides for 5 minutes or until cooked through.

Serves 4

Healthy Banana and Chocolate Milk Shake

For those in a hurry this milk shake provides a complete meal if desired.

2 cups milk
2 bananas, peeled and chopped
2 tblspn honey
1 tblspn unprocessed bran
2 tspn wheatgerm
1 tblspn Milo
1 tspn vanilla essence
2 eggs

1 Place all ingredients in food processor. Blend until smooth.

Serves 2

Tomato Cheese Puffs; Chicken Sausage Sticks

Left: Quick and Yummy Muesli. Above: Dried Fruit Salad with Bananas

Quick and Yummy Muesli

This muesli will keep for several weeks in an airtight container. Serve with milk, yoghurt or fruit juice.

375g (¾lb) packet Kellogg's Bran Flakes

375g (¾lb) packet Kellogg's Allbran

2 cups rolled oats

½ cup pecan nuts, chopped

½ cup dried apricots, chopped

½ cup sultanas

¼ cup dried apples, chopped

1 Combine Bran Flakes, Allbran and rolled oats in a large bowl.

2 Toast pecans on oven tray in moderate oven 5 minutes, cool. Add to cereal.

3 Add dried fruit, mix well. Store in airtight containers.

Makes about 12 cups

Dried Fruit Salad with Bananas

Make ahead if desired. Keep refrigerated.

¼ cup pitted prunes

⅓ cup dried apricots halves

¼ cup sultanas

3 bananas

2 tblspn honey

½ tspn grated lemon rind

15g (½oz) butter, melted

1 cup freshly squeezed orange juice

1 Soak prunes and apricots in water overnight, drain.

2 Place prunes, apricots, sultanas and bananas in ovenproof dish.

3 Combine honey with a little hot water, pour over fruit.

4 Add lemon rind and butter. Bake, covered with foil in moderate oven 35 minutes.

5 Add orange juice, reheat in oven 5 minutes. Serve hot or cold with yoghurt if desired.

Serves 4

Banana Porridge

This porridge is delicious on cold mornings; warm the milk before serving.

1 cup rolled oats

2½ cups boiling water

pinch salt

1 banana, mashed

1 Place oats in pan, add boiling water.

2 Stir until well blended. Add a pinch of salt if desired.

3 Bring to the boil. Boil for 1 minute. Remove from heat. Stir in banana. Serve with milk or yoghurt and honey.

Serves 3-4

Wholemeal Currant Pikelets

1 cup wholemeal self-raising flour

¼ cup raw sugar

⅓ cup currants

1 egg

⅔ cup milk, approximately

1 Sift flour into bowl, return husks to bowl, add sugar and currants. Make a well in centre of dry ingredients, add beaten egg and most of the milk.

2 Beat until smooth. Add enough of remaining milk to give a smooth, pouring consistency. Mixture will thicken on standing.

3 It may be necessary to add a little more milk to the batter as pikelets are being cooked.

4 Drop tablespoonfuls of mixture onto hot greased pan; when bubbles appear on top, turn, cook other side. Serve with butter.

Makes about 20

Hot Spicy Cheese Rolls

2 bread rolls

½ cup grated cheese

1 tblspn sweet fruit chutney

1 tblspn tomato sauce

½ tspn Worcestershire sauce

1 Cut rolls in half.

2 Combine cheese, chutney, tomato sauce and Worcestershire sauce. Pile filling onto base of each roll. Top with other half of bread roll.

3 Wrap in foil or plastic wrap. Bake foil wrapped rolls in moderate oven for 10 minutes or cook plastic wrapped rolls on high in microwave over for 1-2 minutes.

Serves 2

Spaghetti and Ham Omelette

15g (½oz) butter

4 eggs, beaten

1 tblspn water

1 slice ham, chopped

130g (4oz) can spaghetti with tomato and cheese

1 Heat half the butter in frypan. Add half the combined eggs and water.

2 When base sets, sprinkle half the ham and spaghetti over omelette, fold over with a spatula, cook until heated through, gently slide onto a plate.

3 Repeat to make another omelette.

Serves 2

Scrambled Eggs with Corn

15g (½oz) butter

4 eggs, beaten

130g (4oz) can creamed corn

1 tblspn chopped parsley

2 tblspn grated cheese

1 Heat butter in pan, add eggs, creamed corn, parsley and cheese.

2 Cook over medium heat, stirring occasionally until eggs are just scrambled.

3 Serve with hot buttered toast.

Serves 2-4

Spaghetti and Ham Omelette

BABIES AND YOUNG CHILDREN

The little ones in your family should be encouraged to eat well from the earliest months. Here's a selection of good ideas to spark your imagination.

BABY FOOD

Cottage Cheese and Spinach Bake

1 cup cooked spinach

¼ cup red capsicum (pepper), chopped finely

½ cup cottage cheese

2 eggs, lightly beaten

½ cup milk

¼ cup cheddar cheese, grated

1 In a medium bowl combine spinach, capsicum, cottage cheese, eggs and milk; mix well.

2 Pour mixture into 2 x 1½ cup capacity ovenproof dishes, sprinkle with the cheddar cheese.

3 Bake in a moderate oven for 15-20 minutes.

Makes 2

Tomato Pasta with Cheese

1 cup cooked wholewheat pasta

½ 400g (13oz) can peeled tomatoes, drained

1 tblspn low fat cottage cheese

1 In a processor or blender, mix the pasta and tomatoes until chopped finely and well combined.

2 Serve warm with a spoonful of cottage cheese.

Serves 4

Honey Fruit Compote

1 tspn honey

1 apple, peeled and grated

1 banana, mashed

1 ripe pear, mashed

1 Mix the honey in with the fruits and blend well together.

Serves 4

Main picture: Cottage Cheese and Spinach Bake. Above: Tomato Pasta with Cheese

Orange Rice and Honey Compote

1 cup cooked brown rice

1 tblspn honey

1 orange, segmented and chopped

3 tblspn fruit low fat yoghurt

1 Combine rice with honey, orange and yoghurt, mix well.

2 Refrigerate until ready to serve. Decorate with extra fruit if desired.

Serves 4

Cheese and Vegetable Pie

1 cup chopped broccoli

2 medium potatoes, chopped

2 tblspn grated onion

2 medium carrots, chopped

15g (½oz) butter

1 tblspn plain flour

150mls (¼ pint) milk

¼ cup grated cheese

1 egg

pinch nutmeg

¼ cup grated cheese, extra

1 Process broccoli, potatoes, onion and carrots until smooth.

2 Melt butter in pan, add flour, cook 1 minute. Stir in milk, cook, stirring until mixture boils and thickens. Remove from heat, stir in cheese.

3 Add puree of vegetables to cheese sauce. Add egg and nutmeg, mix well.

4 Pour into a greased shallow ovenproof dish, sprinkle with cheese. Bake in moderate oven 30 minutes. Freeze left-overs in portions.

Serves 4

Orange Rice and Honey Compote

Veal Hot Pot

4 veal chops

2 carrots

1 parsnip

3 potatoes

1 cup water

15g (½oz) butter

1 Remove bones, fat and sinew from veal chops, finely chop meat, place into casserole.

2 Peel and finely chop vegetables. Sprinkle carrot and parsnip over veal, top with potato. Pour water over.

3 Bake, covered, in moderate oven 1 hour. Remove lid, dot with butter and bake uncovered further 30 minutes.

Serves 4

Cheese Pudding

1 cup milk

¼ cup wholemeal breadcrumbs

⅓ cup grated cheese

15g (½oz) butter, at room temperature

2 eggs, separated

Fish Pie

1 Stir over a low heat 3 minutes. Cool mixture on a plate before shaping into rissoles. Brush with lightly beaten egg white, toss in breadcrumbs.

3 Heat oil in pan, cook rissoles on both sides until golden, drain on absorbent paper.

Serves 2

Fish Pie

150g (5oz) cooked white fish (boneless fillet)

½ cup mashed potato

¼ cup cooked carrots, mashed

2 tspn chopped parsley

1 tblspn breadcrumbs

1 tblspn butter, melted

1 Flake the fish and discard any bones and skin.

2 Combine mashed potato and carrots, spread half the mixture over the base of a greased oven-proof dish.

3 Arrange fish on top, sprinkle with parsley. Cover with remaining potato.

4 Combine breadcrumbs and butter and sprinkle over the top. Bake in moderate oven for 15 minutes.

Serves 2

Baked Bean and Vegetable Casserole

130g (4oz) baked beans in tomato sauce

1 small carrot, finely chopped

¼ cup finely chopped beans

¼ cup frozen peas

¼ cup grated cheese

1 Combine baked beans and vegetables. Place into small casserole dish, cover and bake in moderate oven 30 minutes.

2 Remove lid, sprinkle with cheese, return to oven for 5 minutes or until cheese is melted.

Serves 1

1 Bring milk to the boil, pour over breadcrumbs in bowl. Stand 5 minutes.

2 Stir in cheese, butter and egg yolks, mix well.

3 Beat egg whites with rotary beater until firm peaks form. Fold into cheese mixture.

4 Divide mixture evenly between four greased oven proof dishes (½ cup capacity). Bake in moderately hot oven 15 minutes or until golden.

Serves 4

Chicken Rissoles

1 cup cooked chicken, finely chopped

30g (1oz) butter

¼ cup instant mashed potato

1 egg, separated

milk

breadcrumbs

oil for frying

1 Melt butter in pan, add chicken, potato and egg yolk and enough milk to make a moist consistency.

Fruity Cheese Log

PLAY LUNCH

Fruity Cheese Log

Make this in advance and keep refrigerated up to a week. This recipe would appeal to gourmet kids.

10 dried apricots, finely chopped

2 tblspn orange juice

250g (½lb) packet cream cheese

½ cup grated cheddar cheese

¼ cup chopped peanuts

¾ cup poppy seeds

1 Soak apricots in orange juice overnight.

2 Blend cream cheese and cheddar cheese together, stir in apricots and juice mixture.

3 Add peanuts, mix well. Refrigerate mixture 1 hour. Roll mixture into log shape about 20cm (8in) long, roll in poppy seeds, cover and refrigerate overnight.

4 Serve with dry crackers, such as wheatmeals or water biscuits.

Serves 4

Lettuce and Ham Rolls

These may be made the night before, if desired.

4 cos or butter lettuce leaves, washed and dried

4 slices ham

2 gherkins, cut in half lengthwise

1 stick celery, cut into 4 x 8cm (1¾ x 3½in) lengths

1 Arrange lettuce leaves on bench in single layer.

2 Top each lettuce leaf with a slice of ham.

3 Place half a gherkin in the groove of each celery stick. Place gherkin and celery along one side of ham and lettuce, roll up and wrap securely in plastic wrap to hold the shape.

4 Repeat with remaining 3 rolls. Place into playlunch bags and seal. Refrigerate until ready to go to school.

Serves 2

Hard-boiled Egg Snack Pack

This will appeal to those kids who feel like savoury food for playlunch that is light but will fill them up until lunchtime.

Celery Boats

Celery Boats

2 hard-boiled eggs

1 Lebanese cucumber, sliced

1 tomato, cut into wedges

2 x 10cm (4in sticks celery)

2 lettuce leaves

1 tblspn mayonnaise

1 Remove shells from eggs, cut in half lengthwise.

2 Place an egg, half the cucumber slices, tomato wedges, a celery stick and a lettuce leaf into a sandwich bag, top with half the mayonnaise, if desired. Seal bag, repeat with remaining ingredients to make another snack pack.

3 Refrigerate until ready to go to school.

Serves 2

Sweet Corn Soup

This soup may be left unblended if desired.

2 rashers bacon, chopped

2 corn cobs, corn removed

1 onion, finely chopped

1 stick celery, chopped

1 potato, peeled, finely chopped

2 tblspn wholemeal plain flour

2 cups milk

2 cups chicken stock

2 tblspn chopped parsley

1 Cook bacon, corn and onion in pan for 5 minutes, add celery and potato, cook 2 minutes.

2 Stir in flour, cook 1 minute. Stir in milk and stock, bring to boil reduce heat, simmer 15 minutes or until vegetables are tender.

3 Puree soup in processor or blender. Reheat in pan, stir in parsley just before serving.

4 Send to school in a thermos.

Serves 4

Celery Boats

2 sticks celery

¼ cup cream cheese

¼ cup peanut butter

sultanas

1 Wash celery and trim ends.

2 Beat cream cheese and peanut butter together, spread along groove in celery.

3 Dot with sultanas. Cut into 5cm (2in) lengths. Place into play-lunch bags and seal.

Serves 2

AFTERNOON TEA

Wholemeal Date Muffins

Prepare the night before for afternoon tea the next day. Freeze any leftover muffins if there are any.

1¼ cups plain flour

½ tspn bicarbonate of soda

½ tspn cinnamon

¼ cup sugar

¾ cup unprocessed bran

60g (2oz) dates, finely chopped

¼ cup oil

¾ cup buttermilk

1 egg, beaten

1 Sift flour into bowl with soda, cinnamon and sugar. Stir in bran and dates.

2 Make a well in centre of dry ingredients, add oil, buttermilk and egg, mix to combine. Cover, refrigerate overnight.

3 Drop tablespoonfuls of mixture into a well-greased deep muffin pan. Bake in moderately hot oven 20 minutes.

4 Serve hot with butter.

Makes 8 muffins

Fruity Slice

This slice keeps for up to one week, if there is any left.

1 cup sugar

250g (½lb) butter

1 cup sultanas

1 cup chopped apricots (same size as sultanas)

2 eggs, beaten

1 cup white self-raising flour

1 cup wholemeal self-raising flour

1 tspn mixed spice

1 Place sugar and butter in saucepan, heat until butter melts.

2 Add sultanas, apricots and eggs. Mix well.

3 Sift flours into a bowl, return husks to bowl.

4 Stir sifted flours and mixed spice into butter fruit mixture.

5 Spread into greased Swiss roll tin. Bake in moderate oven 20 minutes.

6 Cool before cutting into squares. Store in airtight container.

Serves 12

Wholemeal Date Muffins; Fruity Slice

Left: French Toast. Above: Pizza Muffins

French Toast

This is great for winter afternoons. It also makes a good breakfast.

1 egg yolks
¼ cup milk
3 slice wholemeal bread
butter to grease pan

1 Beat egg and milk together with rotary beater.

2 Cut slices of bread in half. Heat greased frypan.

3 Pick up bread with a fork and dip both sides into egg mixture.

4 Cook bread in hot pan. Turn when browned underneath. Cook other side until golden.

5 Serve immediately with honey.

Makes 6 slices

Pizza Muffins

Ideal for hungry ones to fill them up until dinner time.

1 wholegrain muffin, cut in half
butter
1 tblspn tomato paste
½ carrot, grated
½ stick celery, finely chopped
1 slice ham, chopped
½ cup mozzarella cheese

1 Butter each muffin half. Toast under griller until golden.

2 Spread with tomato paste and top with carrot, celery, ham and mozzarella cheese. Place under hot griller until cheese melts. Serve immediately.

Serves 2

Banana Rolls

2 bananas
2 rashers bacon, rind removed
2 tblspn grated cheese

1 Peel bananas, wrap bacon around banana in a spiral. Secure with toothpicks.

2 Cook under a medium grill until bacon is cooked. Sprinkle with cheese and grill 30 seconds or until cheese melts.

3 Remove tooth picks and serve immediately.

Serves 2

WHEN SCHOOLDAYS ARE HAPPY DAYS

It's nice to know when the children are off to school they have something healthy to eat. Later in this chapter, we provide recipes to use when helping out in the school tuckshop.

PACKED LUNCHES

Potato Pie

Wrap potato pie in plastic wrap for lunch boxes. Freeze remaining pie for up to one month.

800g (1½lb) peeled potatoes (about 6 medium potatoes)

15g (½oz) butter

1 onion, finely chopped

2 bacon rashers, finely chopped

1 clove garlic, crushed

1 cup grated cheese

2 tomatoes, sliced

1 Slice potatoes in processor. Arrange one third on base of slice tin.

2 Heat butter in pan, cook onion, bacon and garlic for 5 minutes. Sprinkle one third of this mixture over layer of potatoes.

3 Sprinkle over one third of cheese then a third of the potatoes and a third of the onion mixture. Arrange sliced tomatoes in single layer over onion mixture. Sprinkle with a third of the cheese.

4 Make a final layer of potato, onion mixture and cheese. Bake in moderate oven 40 minutes or until golden, cool and cut into squares.

Serves 4

Hi-Fibre Pasties

These are quick and easy to make and very high in fibre. Make the night before.

2 sheets wholemeal shortcrust pastry

15g (½oz) butter

1 onion, sliced

1 rasher bacon, chopped

1 carrot, chopped

125g (4oz) can baked beans

⅔ cup grated cheese

1 egg, beaten

1 Use an upside down saucer to cut out two rounds of pastry.

2 Heat butter in pan, cook onion, bacon and carrot 5 minutes, cool. Add baked beans and mix well.

3 Divide baked beans mixture between two pastry circles. Pile filling into centre of pastry, sprinkle with cheese. Brush edges with beaten egg, fold over the pastry to form a pastie. Make a fluted pattern to seal pastry.

4 Place pasties onto greased oven tray, brush with beaten egg. Bake in moderate oven 25 minutes or until golden brown. Cool, then refrigerate until ready to take to school.

Makes 2

Hi-Fibre Pasties

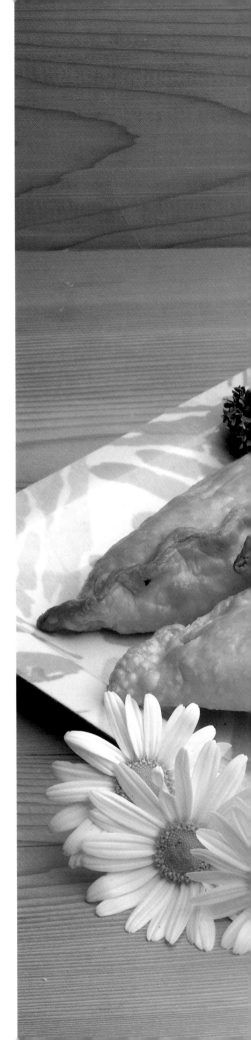

Fruit, Nut and Cheese Salad

Fruit, Nut and Cheese Salad

Use remaining salad for afternoon tea or the next day's lunch.

2 tblspn almonds

1 small red apple (with skin on), chopped

1 small orange, peeled, cut into 2.5cm (1in) cubes.

1 banana, sliced

1 small pear (with skin on), chopped

½ cup chopped cheese (Gouda or Edam)

¼ cup natural yoghurt

1 Toast almonds on oven tray in moderate oven 5 minutes, cool.

2 Combine all ingredients in bowl. Spoon into lunch boxes. Refrigerate until ready to go to school.

Serves 2-4 (depends on appetites)

Tuna and Rice Salad

1½ cups cooked brown rice

220g (7oz) can tuna in brine, drained

15g (½oz) butter

1 onion, chopped

⅓ bunch silverbeet (about 4 leaves) washed, finely chopped

¼ cup grated cheese

¼ cup French dressing

1 Combine rice and tuna in bowl.

2 Heat butter in pan, cook onion 5 minutes or until golden brown. Add to bowl.

3 Boil, steam or microwave silverbeet until tender, drain. Rinse under cold water. Add to bowl with grated cheese and French dressing, toss well.

4 Spoon into lunch boxes. Refrigerate until ready to go to school.

Serves 2-4 (depends on appetites)

Pizza Slice

Pizza Slice

Freeze extra slices or serve for afternoon tea or playlunch.

PASTRY

155g (5oz) plain wholemeal flour

155g (5oz) plain flour

½ tspn salt

1 sachet dried yeast

2 tblspn oil

¾ cup warm water

TOPPING

1 tblspn oil

1 onion, chopped

400g (14oz) can tomatoes, undrained

½ tspn dried oregano

½ tspn dried basil

¼ cup tomato paste

½ cup sliced mushrooms

2 spring onions (scallions), chopped

125g (4oz) ham, chopped

1 tblspn black olives

1 cup grated mozzarella cheese

1 Combine flours, salt and yeast in bowl, stir in oil and warm water. Turn onto a lightly floured surface, knead until smooth and elastic about 10 minutes.

2 Place dough in an oiled bowl, cover with plastic wrap and a teatowel. Stand in a warm place until doubled in size, about 20 minutes (turn oven on low, open oven door, stand bowl on oven door).

3 Knead dough 2 minutes. Roll out to line an oven tray 28 x 35cm (11 x 14in). Heat oil in pan, cook onion 5 minutes, add tomatoes, oregano and basil. Crush tomatoes with spoon. Reduce heat, simmer for 10 minutes, cool.

4 Spread tomato paste over pizza dough, then spread with onion mixture. Sprinkle evenly with mushrooms, spring onions, ham and olives, then mozzarella cheese.

5 Bake in moderately hot oven 20 minutes or until golden.

6 Cut into 12 squares, cool. Wrap squares in plastic wrap.

Serves 6

Sesame Coated Chicken

12 chicken drumsticks and/or wings

1 tblspn tahini

2 tblspn olive oil

1 tblspn sesame oil

1 tblspn tomato paste

2 tblspn sesame seeds

1 Combine tahini, olive and sesame oil, and tomato paste on a plate.

2 Coat the chicken pieces in the mixture, then roll them in sesame seeds.

3 Place onto rack in a baking dish. Bake in moderate oven 40 minutes or until golden brown and cooked through.

4 Cool on rack, then refrigerate until ready to use. Place into lunch boxes, serve with bread and butter and salad.

Serves 4-6 (depends on appetites)

Colourful Pasta Salad

Use whatever ingredients you have in this salad eg. leftover vegetables or cold meat.

2 cups small pasta shapes such as wholemeal macaroni or bow ties.

2 tblspn French dressing

125g (4oz) green beans, chopped

125g (4oz) lean leg ham, chopped

½ small red capsicum (pepper), chopped

4 small radishes, trimmed and sliced

1 spring onion (scallion), finely chopped

1 Cook pasta in large pot of boiling water for 10 minutes or until just tender, drain. Rinse under cold water. Place into bowl with French dressing, toss well.

2 Plunge beans into boiling water 1 minute, drain, rinse under cold water, add to pasta.

3 Add remaining ingredients to pasta, toss well. Refrigerate overnight if possible.

Serves 2

Waldorf and Cottage Cheese Salad

½ cup chopped celery

1 cup chopped red or green apples

1 tblspn chopped walnuts

1 tblspn chopped dates

1 tblspn mayonnaise

125g (4oz) cottage cheese

1 Combine all ingredients in bowl.

2 Spoon into two lunch boxes. Refrigerate until ready to take to school. Serve with buttered bread or biscuits.

Serves 2

Meatloaf Sandwiches

4 slices wholemeal bread

butter

salad — lettuce, tomato, cucumber

MEATLOAF

500g (1lb) lean minced beef

⅓ cup wholegrain bread crumbs

1 onion, minced

2 tblspn chopped parsley

⅓ cup sweet fruit chutney

2 tspn Worcestershire sauce

2 tblspn tomato sauce

½ tspn dried basil

1 egg

Freeze extra Meatloaf or serve for dinner, if desired, and use leftovers for sandwiches.

1 Combine all Meatloaf ingredients in bowl. Mix well.

2 Shape Meatloaf into a loaf shape. Place into baking dish, bake in moderately slow oven 45 minutes.

3 Spread extra chutney on top of loaf. Bake for further 15 minutes. Cool. Cut into 1.5cm (¾in) slices.

Sesame Coated Chicken; Colourful Pasta Salad

4 Make Meatloaf sandwiches with bread, butter and salad. Wrap in plastic wrap ready for lunch boxes.

Makes 2 sandwiches and extra Meatloaf

Wholesome Salad Roll with Chicken Liver Spread

2 wholemeal rolls or pita bread

2 lettuce leaves, shredded

1 tomato, sliced

4 slices beetroot

⅓ cup grated carrot

2 tblspn alfalfa sprouts

1 Lebanese cucumber, sliced

CHICKEN LIVER SPREAD

60g (2oz) butter

1 clove garlic, crushed

250g (½lb) chicken livers

60g (2oz) ham, finely chopped

½ cup chicken stock

2 tblspn tomato paste

The Chicken Liver Spread makes more than you'll need for two rolls. Serve remainder as an afternoon tea snack or starter before a meal with hot buttered toast. Keep refrigerated for up to a week or freeze up to 1 month.

1 Cut rolls or pita bread in half.

2 Spread one side generously with Chicken Liver Spread. Place the salad ingredients on one side of roll and top with other side.

3 Chicken Liver Spread: heat butter in pan, add garlic, chicken livers, ham, stock and tomato paste. Cook 10 minutes. Puree in blender or processor until smooth. Pour into dish, refrigerate 2 hours or until set.

Makes 2 rolls and extra Chicken Liver Spread

Chicken Salad

SCHOOL CANTEEN

Ricotta Cheese and Walnut Sandwiches

500g (1lb) ricotta cheese

1 cup chopped walnuts

1 cup chopped dried apricots

2 loaves wholegrain bread

1 Combine cheese, walnuts and apricots in bowl, mix well.

2 Make sandwiches without butter and a generous amount of filling.

3 Cut sandwiches in half diagonally. Wrap each one in plastic wrap for sale.

Makes 20 sandwiches

Chicken and Apricot Sandwiches

4 cups chopped cooked chicken

2 cups finely chopped celery

2 cups chopped dried apricots

⅔ cups soya mayonnaise

2 loaves brown bread

1 Combine chicken, celery, apricots and mayonnaise in bowl, mix well.

2 Make sandwiches without butter and a generous amount of filling.

3 Cut sandwiches in half diagonally. Wrap each one in plastic wrap for sale.

Makes 20 sandwiches

Chicken Salad

Serve with wholemeal bread

2 cups broccoli flowerets

2 cups chopped, cooked chicken

2 carrots, sliced diagonally

1 avocado, chopped

1 tblspn soy sauce

1 tspn grated ginger

1 tspn sesame oil

¼ cup French dressing

1 Bring a large saucepan of water to the boil. Blanch broccoli for 1 minute, then refresh under cold water.

2 Arrange chicken, broccoli, carrots and avocado; dress with combined soy sauce, ginger, sesame oil and French dressing.

Serves 4-6

Flatbread Pizza

Flatbread Pizza

2 rounds of flatbread

2 tblspn tomato paste

1 cup chopped ham

1 cup grated cheddar cheese

1 tblspn chopped parsley

1 Spread tomato paste over each flatbread round. Sprinkle ham, cheese and parsley on top.

2 Bake in moderate oven 15-20 minutes. Serve on paper plates.

Each round makes 6 slices

Jaffles with Corn, Egg or Tuna

3 loaves buttered brown bread

CORN

200g (6½oz) grated cheese

310g (10oz) can creamed corn

EGG

5 hard-boiled eggs, peeled and chopped

125g (4oz) grated cheese

TUNA

440g (14oz) can tuna, drained, mashed

¼ cup soya mayonnaise

250g (½lb) cheese slices

1 Make corn filling by combining cheese and corn well. Make egg filling by combining eggs and cheese. Make tuna filling by combining tuna and mayonnaise. Use cheese slice on top.

2 Use ¼ cup of corn or egg filling or 2 tablespoons of tuna filling with a slice of cheese to make 30 sandwiches with buttered sides of bread out.

3 Preheat jaffle cooker, cook jaffles 2-3 minutes or until golden. Keep hot in a pie-warmer.

Makes 30 jaffles

Cottage Cheese and Tuna Salad

125g (4oz) creamed cottage cheese

2 x 425g (13½oz) cans tuna, drained

10 tomatoes, finely chopped

¼ cup chopped chives

40-60 wholemeal crispbreads

1 Combine cottage cheese, tuna, tomatoes and chives in bowl; mix well.

2 Spoon into 10 plastic containers, seal with lids.

3 Serve with plastic fork or spoon and 4-6 crispbreads wrapped in plastic wrap.

Makes 10 servings

Frozen Banana Nut Iceblocks

Frozen Banana Nut Iceblocks

5 just-ripe bananas

100g (3½oz) dark chocolate

15g (½oz) copha, melted

10 paddle pop sticks

1 cup finely chopped peanuts

1 Peel bananas and cut in half. Insert wooden paddle pop sticks into each half.

2 Melt chocolate in a heatproof bowl over hot water. Remove from heat, add copha; mix well.

3 Brush each banana with the chocolate mixture. Roll in the chopped nuts and freeze, covered until serving.

Makes 10

Satay Chicken

500g (1lb) chicken breast fillet

1 tblspn oil

2 tblspn crunchy peanut butter

1 tblspn light, low salt, soy sauce

¼ tspn ground cumin

wooden satay sticks

1 Slice chicken fillets into 2cm (¾in) cubes, thread onto satay sticks (about 5 cubes per satay).

2 In a small bowl combine oil, peanut butter, soy sauce and cumin; mix well.

3 Brush each satay with the peanut butter mixture, refrigerate 30 minutes.

4 Grill each satay 2 minutes each side, or until chicken is cooked. Serve with brown rice.

Makes about 10 kebabs

Satay Chicken; Potato and Egg Salad

Potato and Egg Salad

2 bacon rashers, chopped

500g (1lb) baby new potatoes, halved

4 hard-boiled eggs, sliced

1 red capsicum (pepper), chopped

1 stick celery, chopped

1 tblspn soya mayonnaise

1 tblspn light sour cream

2½ tblspn French dressing

2 tspn chopped chives

2 tspn chopped basil

2 tspn chopped parsley

1 Cook bacon until crisp. Cook potatoes until just tender.

2 In a large bowl combine potatoes, eggs, capsicum and celery.

3 In a small bowl mix mayonnaise, sour cream, French dressing and herbs.

4 Pour dressing over salad, sprinkle with crisp bacon pieces.

Serves 4

Peanut, Cheese and Carrot Spread Sandwiches

½ cup smooth peanut butter

1 cup grated cheddar cheese

½ cup grated carrot

2 loaves raisin bread

1 Combine peanut butter, cheese and carrot in bowl, mix well.

2 Make sandwiches without butter. Use two teaspoons of the spread per sandwich. Cut into half diagonally. Wrap each one in plastic wrap for sale.

Makes about 20 sandwiches

SEAFOOD, FISH AND CHICKEN

These ingredients are packed with nourishment for growing bodies and active minds. By encouraging a taste for fish and chicken you're helping form good eating habits for later on.

FISH AND SHELLFISH

Ocean Perch in an Oven Bag

Ocean perch has almost no bones or skin so it is ideal for kids.

2 ocean perch fillets

2 tspn mild mustard

1 spring onion (scallion), finely chopped

1 orange, rind grated, juice squeezed

1 tomato, sliced

15g (½oz) butter

1 Trim any remaining skin or bones from fish. Arrange in oven bag in single layer.

2 Spread each fillet with mustard. Sprinkle with spring onion, grated orange rind and juice.

3 Arrange tomato slices on top. Dot with butter. Seal bag, place in shallow ovenproof dish.

4 Bake in moderate oven 20 minutes. Open bag, use a spatula to lift fish with topping onto plates. Serve with sliced jacket potatoes, brown rice or salad.

Serves 2

Fish with Corn

4-6 snapper cutlets

1 piece corn on the cob or 350g (11oz) can sweetcorn

1 tspn arrowroot or cornflour

½ cup vegetable or tomato juice

1 tblspn oil

2 tblspn chopped parsley

1 Remove corn from cob with a knife. Boil, steam or microwave corn until tender, drain. Blend or process with arrowroot and vegetable juice.

2 Brush cutlets with oil on both sides. Cook under a hot grill 2 minutes, turn over, grill further 1 minute. Pour over corn mixture.

3 Grill for a further 10 minutes or until cutlets are cooked through and corn mixture thickens slightly and browns on top. Serve sprinkled with parsley. Serve with a salad.

Serves 4-6

Ocean Perch in an Oven Bag

Salmon and Brown Rice Mornay

This recipe will appeal to the whole family.

1½ cups cooked brown rice

1 onion, finely chopped

2 eggs, beaten

15g (½oz) butter, melted

400g (13oz) can salmon

2 cups milk

¼ cup cornflour

1 tspn curry powder

1 tspn dry mustard

1 tspn paprika

⅓ cup grated cheese

2 tblspn chopped parsley

1 tblspn lemon juice

¼ cup fresh breadcrumbs

2 tblspn grated cheese, extra

1 Combine rice, onion, one well-beaten egg and melted butter. Mix well and spread over base of 18cm x 28cm (7 x 11in) slab tin.

2 Drain salmon and reserve the liquid for the sauce. Press salmon evenly over rice.

3 Combine milk, cornflour, curry powder, mustard and paprika in saucepan. Cook, stirring until mixture boils and thickens. Add salmon liquid, cheese, parsley, lemon juice and remaining well beaten egg.

4 Pour sauce over salmon. Sprinkle with combined breadcrumbs and extra cheese. Bake in moderate oven 40 minutes.

5 Serve with a salad.

Serve 4

Above: Tuna Fish Fingers

Barbecued Prawns (Shrimp)

Adults will love these as much as the kids.

500g (1lb) green king prawns (shrimp)

2 tspn sesame oil

1 tblspn tamari or shoyu (see note)

1 tblspn oil

1 tspn honey

1 clove garlic, crushed

1 Peel prawns but leave tails on. Thread onto bamboo skewers.

2 Combine remaining ingredients in dish. Use a brush to paint mixture onto prawns on both sides.

3 Cook on barbecue or under griller on both sides until just tender. Be careful not to overcook them. Brush with remaining oil mixture during cooking. Serve with salad and rice.

Note: Tamari or shoyu are available in some supermarkets and health-food shops.

Serves 4

Tuna Fish Fingers

Freeze fish fingers for up to one month if desired.

220g (7oz) can tuna, drained, mashed

2 medium potatoes, boiled and mashed

2 tblspn chopped parsley

1 tblspn tamari or shoyu (see note)

1 tblspn chutney

1 egg, beaten

1 cup wholemeal breadcrumbs

1 Combine tuna, potatoes, parsley, tamari and chutney. Gradually add enough egg to make a moist but not over-soft mixture.

2 Divide mixture evenly into 10 pieces. Form into 1.25cm (½in) thick rectangular 'fingers'. Coat in breadcrumbs.

3 Bake on an oventray in moderate oven for 10 minutes or until golden. Alternately, grill or shallow fry on both sides until golden.

4 Serve with a salad.

Serves 4

Salmon and Brown Rice Mornay; Barbecued Prawns (Shrimp)

Chicken and Apple Casserole

The whole family will like this.

1 size 14 (3lb) chicken
1 tblspn oil
1 onion, sliced
1 green apple, peeled, cored, sliced
2 tspn French mustard
2 tspn cornflour
⅔ cup apple juice
1 cup chicken stock
½ cup dry white wine
1 tblspn soy sauce
2 tspn Worcestershire sauce
2 tblspn chopped parsley

1 Cut chicken into 8 pieces. Remove skin and visible fat.

2 Heat oil in pan, cook onion 5 minutes, stirring occasionally. Add apple, cook until soft.

3 Remove onion and apple mixture to casserole dish. Add chicken to pan, brown lightly all over. Add to casserole.

4 Add mustard, combined cornflour and apple juice and remaining ingredients. Cook until mixture boils and thickens. Pour into casserole dish, mix well.

5 Bake, covered, in moderate oven 1 hour. Serve with brown rice and salad.

Serves 4

Mild Chicken Curry with Coconut

Make this for a family meal.

1 size 14 (3lb) chicken
1 tblspn oil
1 onion, sliced
1 tspn curry powder
1 clove garlic, crushed
1 tspn cumin powder
1 tspn turmeric
2 tblspn crunchy peanut butter
¼ cup tomato paste
150g (5oz) can coconut cream
2 cups chicken stock

1 Cut chicken into 8 pieces. Remove skin and visible fat.

2 Heat oil in pan, cook onion 5 minutes; stirring occasionally. Add curry, garlic, cumin and turmeric, cook 1 minute.

3 Add chicken, cook few minutes on each side until light brown. Add remaining ingredients, mix well.

4 Pour into casserole dish, cover, bake in moderate oven 1 hour. Serve with brown rice and salad.

Serves 4

Mild Chicken Curry with Coconut

Tomato Chicken with Olives

Make this for the whole family.

1 size 14 (3lb) chicken
1 tblspn oil
1 onion, chopped
1 clove garlic, crushed
400g (13oz) can tomatoes, undrained
¼ cup dry white wine
½ tspn dried oregano
½ tspn dried basil
1 cup chicken stock
¼ cup black olives

1 Cut chicken into 8 pieces. Remove skin and visible fat.

2 Heat oil in pan, cook onion 5 minutes; stirring occasionally.

3 Remove onion to ovenproof dish. Add chicken to pan, brown lightly on all sides.

4 Add chicken to onions in ovenproof dish. Add remaining ingredients, mix well. Cover, bake in moderate oven 1 hour. Serve with brown rice and salad.

Serves 4

Chinese Chicken

Use leftovers in lunch boxes.

16 chicken drumsticks
¼ cup honey
¼ cup low salt soy sauce
¼ cup dry sherry
pinch five-spice powder

1 Remove skin and visible fat from drumsticks.

2 Combine honey, soy, sherry and five-spice powder in shallow oven proof dish.

3 Coat drumsticks well in mixture. Cover and marinate 2 hours.

Tomato Chicken with Olives;
Chinese Chicken

Mango Chicken

4 Bake in moderate oven 45 minutes. Turn half way through cooking time. Serve with jacket potatoes and salad.

Serves 4

Mango Chicken

1 size 14 (3lb) chicken
1 tblspn oil
2 onions, sliced
425g (13½oz) can mango, drained, pureed
pinch grated nutmeg
3 strips lemon rind
2 tspn cornflour
1½ cups of chicken stock
1 tblspn lemon juice
½ cup natural yoghurt

1 Cut chicken into 8 pieces. Remove skin and visible fat.

2 Heat oil in pan, cook onions 5 minutes; stirring occasionally.

3 Add chicken, brown lightly all over. Add mango, nutmeg, lemon rind, combined cornflour and stock and lemon juice. Cook, stirring until mixture boils and thickens.

4 Pour into casserole dish, bake in moderate oven, covered, 1 hour. Stir in yoghurt. Reheat in oven 5 minutes. Serve with brown rice and salad.

Serves 4

EGGS AND CHEESE TO THE RESCUE

With these handy stand-by ingredients in your kitchen, you will always be able to create economical and healthy meals for active young appetites.

Vegetable Filo Pie

1 onion, peeled

1 potato, peeled

2 carrots, peeled

2 zucchinis (courgettes)

155g (5oz) feta cheese

155g (5oz) cottage cheese

1 cup grated cheddar cheese

2 eggs, lightly beaten

8 sheets filo pastry

60g (2oz) butter, melted

1 Add onion, potato, carrots and zucchini to food processor, process until finely chopped. Boil, steam or microwave vegetables until tender (approx 2 minutes on high). Cool, squeeze out as much excess water as possible from vegetables.

2 Combine cheeses and eggs in large bowl; add vegetable mixture; mix well.

3 Brush each sheet of pastry with butter. Line the base of a greased 23cm (9in) flan dish with 4 sheets of pastry, bringing up around sides. Pour vegetable filling into flan and top with the remaining filo pastry. Trim pastry, leaving about 3cm (1¼ in) edge of dish; roll down to neaten edge. Bake in moderate oven 40 minutes.

Serves 6

Corn and Ham Quiche

Leftover quiche is great for the lunch boxes.

1 sheet wholemeal shortcrust pastry

130g (4oz) can corn kernels, drained

100g (3½oz) ham, chopped

3 spring onions (scallion), finely chopped

¾ cup grated cheese

¾ cup light sour cream

½ cup milk

3 eggs

1 Line a 23cm (9in) flan tin with pastry. Cover pastry with greaseproof paper, fill with dry beans or rice. Bake in moderately hot oven 5 minutes, remove beans and paper, bake further 10 minutes.

2 Combine corn, ham, spring onions and cheese together in a bowl. Beat light sour cream, milk and eggs together in bowl.

3 Spread corn mixture over pastry, pour over egg mixture. Bake in moderate oven for about 30 minutes or until golden brown and set. Serve with salad.

Serves 4-6

Above: Corn and Ham Quiche

3 Lightly beat the eggs and pour them over the vegetables, sprinkle with cheese. Cook over a medium heat for about 2 minutes. When lightly browned use two spatulas to turn the frittata to brown the other side.

4 Cut into wedges. Serve with a salad.

Serves 4

Cheesy Vegetable Slice

1 onion, finely chopped
2 medium potatoes, grated
2 small carrots, grated
2 small zucchini, grated
250g (½lb) feta cheese, crumbled
125g (4oz) cheddar cheese, grated
6 sheets filo pastry
60g (2oz) butter
2 eggs, beaten

1 Combine onion, potatoes, carrots and zucchini in bowl.

2 Add feta and cheddar cheese, mix well.

3 Fold each sheet of pastry to form a rough square; cover with greaseproof paper, then a damp cloth, stand until required. Place a piece of folded pastry in greased baking dish, base measure 23cm x 28cm, (9in x 11in).

4 Brush lightly with melted butter; repeat process with two more folded sheets, brush butter between each sheet.

5 Press vegetable cheese mixture onto pastry. Beat eggs until frothy, pour evenly over vegetables.

6 Cover with remaining three folded sheets of pastry, brushing between each layer with melted butter. Brush top with melted butter.

7 Cut into squares. Bake in moderate oven 35 minutes or until light golden brown. Serve hot.

Serves 4

Below: Cheesy Vegetable Slice

Frittata with Asparagus, Ham and Potato

This is a variation of a Spanish omelette.

1 tblspn oil
1 onion, finely chopped
100g (3½oz) ham, chopped
1 medium potato, grated
340g (11oz) can asparagus, drained, chopped
6 eggs
½ cup grated cheese

1 Heat oil in pan, cook onion, ham and potato gently for 10 minutes.

2 Add asparagus, cook until liquid has evaporated.

MEAT DISHES FOR VARIETY

Lamb, beef, pork and veal provide good nutrition as long as these ingredients are prepared correctly. In the following pages you'll find plenty of recipes that will have the children asking for more.

LAMB

Sweet and Spicy Lamb Casserole

A good dish for the whole family.

1kg (2lb) lamb chops

2 onions

4cm (1¾in) piece green ginger, peeled

2 cloves garlic, peeled

1 tblspn oil

1 tspn curry powder

1 tspn cumin powder

1 tspn coriander powder

1 cup beef stock

⅓ cup sweet fruit chutney

400g (13oz) can tomatoes, undrained.

1 green capsicum (pepper), chopped

1 carrot, chopped

1 stick celery chopped

¼ cup tomato paste

1 Remove excess fat from chops. Cut into 2cm (¾in) cubes.

2 Blend or process onion, ginger and garlic until smooth. Heat oil in pan, cook mixture 5 minutes; stirring occasionally.

3 Add curry, cumin and coriander, cook 1 minute.

4 Place onion mixture in casserole dish with lamb and remaining ingredients, mix well. Bake covered in moderate oven 2 hours.

5 Serve with brown rice.

Serves 4-6

Oat-Coated Lamb Cutlets

8 lamb cutlets

1 cup minute oats

2 tblspn Parmesan cheese

1 tspn dried mixed herbs

3 tblspn oil

2 eggs, beaten

1 Trim excess fat from lamb.

2 Combine oats, Parmesan, herbs and oil.

3 Dip cutlets in beaten egg then oat mixture to coat completely.

4 Place a wire rack in a baking dish. Place coated cutlets on rack. Bake in moderately hot oven 30 minutes or until golden brown.

5 Serve with steamed vegetables.

Serves 4

Barbecued Lamb Kebabs

1kg (2lb) lamb chops

¼ cup olive oil

¼ cup lemon juice

2 onions, minced in processor

2 bay leaves

2 tspn dried oregano

2 tomatoes, pureed

1 Trim excess fat from lamb. Cut into 2cm (¾in) cubes.

Oat-Coated Lamb Cutlets; Minted Racks of Lamb

2 Combine remaining ingredients in dish. Add lamb, mix well. Marinate 2 hours.

3 Drain lamb cubes, thread onto skewers. Barbecue kebabs 3-4 minutes each side, brushing with marinade as they cook. Serve with jacket potatoes and salad.

Serves 4

Devilled Lamb Chops

1kg (2lb) loin chops	
1 tblspn oil	
½ cup water	
2 tspn curry powder	
1 tspn soy sauce	
½ cup sweet fruit chutney	
1 tspn dry mustard	
1 tblspn brown sugar	

1 Trim excess fat from lamb.

2 Combine remaining ingredients in a shallow ovenproof dish. Coat lamb chops in mixture on both sides.

3 Bake, uncovered, in moderate oven 45 minutes. Serve with steamed baby new potatoes and other vegetables.

Serves 4

Minted Racks of Lamb

A great dish for the whole family.

4 baby racks of lamb	
2 tblspn mango chutney	
2 tspn French mustard	
1 clove garlic, crushed	
2 tspn lemon juice	
½ cup chopped mint	
500g (1lb) new potatoes, chopped	

1 Trim excess fat from lamb. Combine chutney, mustard, garlic and lemon juice in bowl.

2 Spread over back of each lamb rack, then sprinkle thickly with chopped mint. Press gently with your hand.

3 Bake in baking dish surrounded by chopped new potatoes in moderate oven 40 minutes or until tender. Serve with steamed vegetables.

Serves 4

Beef in Red Wine

Even little children love this dish.

1kg (2lb) chuck steak

1 tblspn oil

2 bacon rashers, chopped

1 clove garlic, crushed

¼ cup wholemeal plain flour

2 tblspn oil, extra

2 cups red wine

2 cups beef stock

¼ cup tomato paste

250g (½lb) button mushrooms, wiped

2 tblpsn chopped parsley

1 Remove excess fat from beef. Cut into 2cm (¾in) cubes.

2 Heat oil in pan, cook bacon and onion 5 minutes; stirring occasionally, add garlic, cook 1 minute. Place this mixture into casserole dish.

3 Place beef cubes and flour in plastic bag, shake well to coat. Heat oil in pan, cook beef in batches until lightly browned, add to casserole dish.

4 Add wine to hot pan, stir well, scraping up pan juices, add stock and tomato paste, mix well; pour over beef in casserole, mix well.

5 Bake, covered, in moderate oven 1½ hours. Add mushrooms, bake further 15 minutes. Stir in parsley and serve with brown rice and salad.

Serves 6

Chinese Beef Stir-fry

500g (1lb) beef fillet

1 clove garlic, crushed

3 tspn cornflour

1 tspn soy sauce

2 tblspn oil

3 sticks celery, sliced

1 small carrot, sliced

1 tblspn tomato sauce

1 tspn Worcestershire sauce

2 tblspn water

1 chicken stock cube

1 tblspn hoisin sauce

3 tspn barbecue sauce

1 Cut beef into 0.5cm (¼in) slices. Combine garlic, cornflour and soy sauce in bowl, add beef, mix well, stand 20 minutes.

2 Heat pan, add oil, when oil is hot, add beef and cook over high heat until golden brown.

3 Add celery and carrot, cook further 1 minute, remove from pan.

4 Add remaining ingredients to pan, stir over high heat until sauce boils and thickens. Add beef and vegetable mixture, mix well. Serve with brown rice.

Serves 4

Chinese Beef Stir-Fry; Sweet and Sour Meatballs

Sweet and Sour Meatballs

Kids love meatballs.

500g (1lb) lean topside mince

¼ cup sweet fruit chutney

2 tblspn wholemeal plain flour

3 tblspn oil

1 small onion, finely chopped

1 green capsicum (pepper), finely chopped

1 tblspn cornflour

1 tblspn soy sauce

1 tblspn vinegar

2 tblspn brown sugar

440g (14oz) can unsweetened pineapple pieces, undrained

½ cup juice drained from can

1 Combine mince and chutney, shape into about 16 meatballs. Roll meatballs in flour.

2 Heat 2 tablespoons of the oil in pan, brown meatballs in oil, turning often for about 20 minutes. Drain on absorbent paper.

3 Heat remaining 1 tablespoon of oil in saucepan, cook onion and capsicum 5 minutes; stirring occasionally. Add combined cornflour and soy sauce, vinegar, brown sugar, pineapple pieces and juice to pan.

4 Cook, stirring, until mixture boils and thickens, simmer 2 minutes.

5 Pour sauce over meatballs. Serve with brown rice.

Serves 4

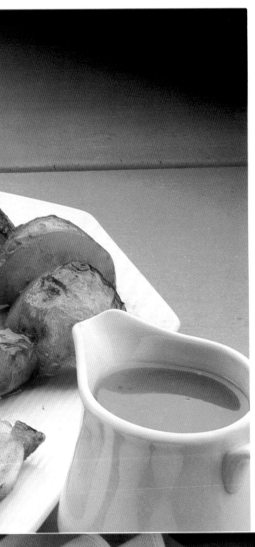

PORK, VEAL AND OFFAL

Honey Glazed Loin of Pork

1 loin of pork to feed 4 people

pinch five-spice powder

⅓ cup honey

1½ tblspn soy sauce

⅓ cup orange juice

1 tspn grated green ginger

1 tspn cornflour

2 tblspn water

1 Remove excess fat and rind from pork. Place pork on rack in baking dish, rub five-spice powder into pork. Bake in moderate oven 1½ hours.

2 Pour combined honey, soy sauce, orange juice and ginger over pork, bake further 20 minutes, spooning sauce over occasionally until rack is cooked through.

3 Remove pork from baking dish, keep warm. Strain pan juices into a small pan, stand a few minutes then skim off all fat. Add blended cornflour and water, stir over heat until sauce boils and thickens.

4 Serve with baked vegetables.

Serves 4

Spicy Apricot Pork Fillets

500g (1lb) pork fillets

2 tspn cornflour

2 tspn soy sauce

1 clove garlic, crushed

2 tspn grated green ginger

425g (13½oz) apricot nectar

½ tspn chilli sauce (optional)

1 Place pork fillets in shallow ovenproof dish. Blend cornflour with soy sauce, garlic, ginger, apricot nectar and chilli sauce.

2 Pour over pork fillets. Bake uncovered in moderate oven 30 minutes.

3 Serve with steamed vegetables and brown rice.

Serves 4

Parsley Brains

4 sets lambs brains

30g (1oz) butter

2 tblspn plain flour

1 cup milk

2 tblspn chopped parsley

1 Place brains in bowl, cover with water, stand 1 hour; drain, peel away membrane. Place brains in pan, cover with cold water, bring to boil, reduce heat, simmer, uncovered 4 minutes, drain.

2 Heat butter in pan, add flour, cook 2 minutes. Gradually stir in milk, cook sauce until mixture boils and thickens. Stir in parsley.

3 Add brains, reheat gently before serving. Serve with potatoes and vegetables or salad.

Serves 4

Main picture: Honey Glazed Loin of Pork; Spicy Apricot Pork Fillets. Above: Parsley Brains

Liver and Bacon

An old favourite, full of iron.

500g (1lb) lamb liver

30g (1oz) butter

2 rashers bacon

1 onion, sliced

½ cup plain flour

1 cup water

1 Cut liver across in slices. Remove large membranes.

2 Heat butter in pan, cook bacon and onion 5 minutes, stirring occasionally.

3 Coat liver in flour, shake off excess. Add liver to pan, cook both sides until just cooked through. Do not overcook. Remove to heated plates.

4 Over high heat add water, cook, stirring until mixture boils and thickens to form a gravy. Pour over liver. Serve with rice and salad.

Serves 4

Veal with Mushroom Sauce

6 veal steaks (escalopes)

2 tblspn oil

500g (1lb) button mushrooms, halved

1 onion, sliced

1 cup beef stock

2 tspn cornflour

1 tblspn water

⅓ cup light sour cream

1 Heat oil in pan, cook veal until lightly browned on each side, remove from pan, keep warm.

2 Add mushrooms and onion to pan, cook 5 minutes, stirring to scrape up pan juices.

3 Add stock, bring to the boil. Add combined cornflour and water. Cook until mixture boils again and thickens. Stir in light sour cream, reheat without boiling. Serve with steamed vegetables.

Serves 6

Glazed Roast Veal

1 kg (2lb) nut of veal

1 tblspn brandy

2 tblspn brown sugar

1 tblspn honey

1 tspn grated lemon rind

1 tblspn chopped parsley

1 cup water

1½ tblspn red currant jelly

1 tblspn lemon juice

1 tspn cornflour

1 tblspn water, extra

1 Combine brandy, brown sugar, honey, lemon rind and parsley in bowl, spread over meat. Place meat in baking dish with ¼ cup of water.

2 Bake in hot oven 15 minutes, reduce heat to moderate, bake further 45 minutes or until tender.

3 Remove meat from baking dish, keep warm. Place baking dish over heat, stir in remaining water, scraping in bits that cling to bottom of dish. Continue stirring until mixture boils. Add red currant jelly and lemon juice, stir until combined.

4 Stir in combined cornflour and extra water, stir until sauce boils and thickens. Serve with sliced veal and steamed vegetables.

Serves 6

Glazed Roast Veal

Veal Paprika

A good dish for when relatives are over for dinner.

3 tblspn oil
2 onions, chopped
1 clove garlic, crushed
1 tblspn paprika
2 tspn French mustard
1½ cups beef stock
¼ cup chopped parsley
1kg (2lb) veal chops
½ cup wholemeal plain flour
2 tblspn slivered almonds
125g (4oz) button mushrooms
200g (6oz) carton natural yoghurt or light sour cream

1 Heat 1 tablespoon of oil in pan, cook onions 5 minutes, stirring occasionally. Add garlic, paprika and mustard, cook 1 minute.

2 Add stock and parsley, mix well, pour into casserole dish.

3 Trim excess fat from veal. Dip veal into flour. Heat remaining 2 tablespoons of oil in pan, cook veal until lightly browned on both sides. Drain on absorbent paper.

4 Add veal chops to casserole dish, bake, covered in moderate oven 1 hour.

5 Meanwhile, toast almonds on oven tray in moderate oven 5 minutes. Add to veal with mushrooms, bake further 15 minutes.

6 Stir in yoghurt, reheat in oven before serving. Serve with noodles or brown rice and salad.

Serves 6

Osso Bucco

750g (1½lb) veal shanks, knuckles or chops

1 tblspn oil

2 onions, chopped

2 carrots, chopped

2 stick celery, chopped

2 cloves garlic, crushed

wholemeal plain flour

2 tblspn oil, extra

2 x 400g (13oz) cans tomatoes, undrained

½ cup dry red wine

2 cups beef stock

1 tspn dried basil

1 tspn dried thyme

1 bay leaf

1 strip lemon peel

1 Heat oil in pan, cook onion, carrots and celery 10 minutes; stirring occasionally. Add garlic. Transfer vegetables to shallow ovenproof dish.

2 Coat veal in flour, heat extra oil in pan, cook veal until lightly browned all over. Arrange veal over vegetables in ovenproof dish.

3 Add tomatoes to pan in which veal was cooked and add wine, stock, herbs and lemon rind. Bring to the boil, scraping up pan juices. Pour over veal.

4 Bake, covered, in moderate oven 1½ hours or until veal is tender. Serve with brown rice and salad.

Serves 6

Veal with Tomato and Cheese

A good dish to make for guests.

500g (1lb) thin veal steaks (about 5 medium steaks)

1 egg, beaten

1 cup wholemeal breadcrumbs

¼ cup grated Parmesan cheese

¼ cup oil

1 small onion, finely chopped

400g (13oz) can tomatoes, undrained

¼ tspn dried basil

½ chicken stock cube

1 tblspn tomato paste

1 clove garlic, crushed

2 tblspn dry white wine

small strip lemon peel

6 slices mozzarella cheese

1 Beat veal steaks until very thin or ask your butcher to do it for you.

2 Dip veal into egg then coat in combined breadcrumbs and Parmesan cheese.

3 Heat 2 tablespoons of the oil in pan, cook veal until golden brown on both sides. Drain on absorbent paper. Arrange veal in single layer in lightly greased shallow ovenproof dish.

4 Heat remaining tablespoon of oil in saucepan, cook onion 5 minutes, stirring occasionally. Add tomatoes and remaining ingredients except the cheese. Cook slowly for 5 minutes. Puree mixture in blender or processor until smooth.

5 Pour tomato sauce mixture over veal, top with cheese slices. Bake in moderate oven 10-15 minutes or until cheese melts and veal heated through.

Serves 4-6

Osso Bucco; Veal with Tomato and Cheese

Good Eating
What Your Children Need

FOOD GROUP	THEY PROVIDE	MINIMUM DAILY AMOUNTS
Bread, cereals.	carbohydrate for energy, fibre, protein, vitamins and minerals.	4-6 servings — 1 slice bread or small bowl breakfast cereal or ½ cup pasta or rice.
Vegetables, fruits.	Vitamins and fibre.	4-6 servings — 1 piece fruit or ½ cup vegetable.
Fish, seafood, poultry, meat, eggs, dried peas and beans, lentils, nuts, peanut butter and seeds.	Protein, vitamins and minerals.	2 servings — 100g (3½oz) meat or ¾ cup cooked beans.
Milk, cheese, yoghurt.	Minerals and vitamins Protein.	600mls (1 pint) or 40g (1½oz) cheese and 200g (6½oz) yoghurt.
Butter, margarine or oil.	Vitamins, fat.	1-2 tablespoons.

A typical day's meals may be as follows:

Breakfast — bowl of cereal and milk.
piece of toast with butter and vegemite.

Playlunch — yoghurt or glass milk.
slice of bread and butter.

Lunch — sandwich with butter, egg and salad and a piece of fruit.

Afternoon tea — piece of fruit.
slice of bread and butter and cheese.

Dinner — fish dish with three vegetables
eg. fillet of boneless white fish or BBQ prawns
eg. potato, carrot and broccoli

Ring The Changes With Side Dishes

Ringing the changes can be a headache when cooking for your family. But variety is important for enjoyment as well as for good eating. These "extra" dishes provide plenty of inspiration.

Avocado Salad

2 avocados

1 tomato

1 red capsicum (pepper)

1 Lebanese cucumber

8 black olives

1 tblspn lemon juice

1 Cut avocados in half. Carefully remove skin, cut avocados into 2cm (¾in) cubes.

2 Cut tomato, capsicum and cucumber into 2cm (¾in) cubes. Combine avocado and all other ingredients in salad bowl, toss well.

Serves 4

Sprout Salad

2 cups mixed sprouts

1 cup green grapes

1 cup grated carrot

½ cup chopped red capsicum (pepper)

2 tblspn chopped parsley

1 tblspn chopped chives

½ cup soya mayonnaise

lettuce

1 Combine all ingredients in bowl.

2 Serve salad on lettuce leaves.

Serves 4

Green Salad with Pecans

1 lettuce

125g (4oz) snow peas

4 radishes

1 stick celery, sliced

⅓ cup pecan nuts

¼ cup olive oil

1 tblspn wine vinegar

1 tblspn rice wine vinegar

pinch dried oregano leaves

pinch dried basil leaves

1 Wash and dry lettuce, shred roughly. Top and tail snow peas. Boil, steam or microwave snow peas 1 minute, drain. Cool under cold running water until cold, drain.

2 Combine lettuce, radishes, snow peas and celery in salad bowl. Toast pecan nuts on oven tray in moderate oven 5 minutes, cool. Add to salad.

3 Combine remaining ingredients in a screw-top jar, shake well, pour over salad, toss well.

Serves 4

Avocado Salad; Green Salad with Pecans

Green Beans with Sesame Seeds

250g (½lb) green beans

2 tspn olive oil

1 tblspn sesame seeds

2 tspn soy sauce

1 Top and tail beans. Cut into 3cm (1¼in) diagonal slices.

2 Heat oil in pan, add sesame seeds, cook, stirring, until light golden.

3 Add beans, stir-fry 2 minutes or until bright green. Add soy sauce and serve immediately.

Serves 4

Broccoli and Cauliflower Salad

1 cup broccoli flowerets

1 cup cauliflower flowerets

½ cup grated cheese

½ cup French dressing

2 tblspn flaked almonds

1 Boil, steam or microwave broccoli and cauliflower until just tender, drain. Run under cold running water until vegetables are cold.

2 Combine vegetables in bowl with cheese and dressing.

3 Toast almonds on oven tray in moderate oven for 5 minutes, cool. Sprinkle almonds over salad.

Serves 4

Sweet Potato with Bacon and Cumin

2 orange sweet potatoes (Kumera)

1 bacon rasher

15g butter

pinch ground cumin

1 Peel sweet potato, cut into sticks or chunks. Boil, steam or microwave sweet potato until tender, drain.

2 Meanwhile, remove rind and excess fat from bacon. Cook finely chopped bacon in pan until crisp.

3 Add drained sweet potato to pan, add butter and cumin. Toss gently.

Serves 4

Crispy Potatoes

4 large washed potatoes

1 tblspn oil

2 tblspn Parmesan cheese

1 Cut potatoes in half lengthwise.

2 Using a sharp knife carefully make cuts about 3mm (1/8in) apart from top nearly through to flat base.

3 Place flat side down on oiled oven tray, brush with oil. Bake in moderately hot oven 50 minutes or until crisp.

4 Sprinkle with cheese, return to oven 2 minutes or until melted.

Serves 4

Main picture: Sweet Potato with Bacon and Cumin; Crispy Potatoes. Above: Green Beans with Sesame Seeds

Thai Vegetable Stir-fry

1 tblspn oil

1 carrot, cut into thin strips

3 spring onions (scallions), sliced diagonally

125g (4oz) green beans, sliced diagonally

1 bunch fresh asparagus, sliced diagonally in 5cm (2in) length

60g (2oz) snow peas

1 tspn grated fresh ginger

1 tblspn dry sherry

1 tspn cornflour

½ cup chicken stock

1 tblspn fish sauce

½ tspn sesame oil

1 cup bean sprouts

1 Heat the oil in a large pan or wok. Add the carrot strips, spring onions, beans, asparagus, snow peas and ginger, stir-fry for 3 minutes.

2 Add combined blended sherry and cornflour, stock, fish sauce and sesame oil, toss in sprouts and stir-fry another 1-2 minutes.

Serves 4

Macaroni with Lemon and Dill

250g (½lb) wholemeal macaroni

1 cup milk

¼ cup lemon juice

1 tspn grated lemon rind

2 tblspn chopped fresh dill

1 Put the milk, lemon juice and lemon rind in a large frying pan. Bring to the boil, reduce heat, simmer 3 minutes.

2 Add macaroni and enough water to almost cover. Simmer, covered, stirring occasionally until macaroni is tender, about 15 minutes. If necessary, add more water to prevent macaroni sticking.

Thai Vegetable Stir-Fry

3 Stir in dill and serve immediately.

Serves 4

Corn with Peas

2 corn cobs, corn removed

1 cup peas

2 tspn soy sauce

2 tspn butter

1 Remove corn from the cob with a sharp knife.

2 Boil, steam or microwave corn and peas until tender, drain. Add soy sauce and butter, toss well.

Serves 4

Jacket Potatoes with Almond Filling

4 medium sized old potatoes

250g (½lb) broccoli

1 carrot, finely chopped

1 tblspn soy mayonnaise

2 tspn lemon juice

½ cup grated cheese

⅓ cup slivered almonds

1 tspn paprika

1 Scrub and dry potatoes, pierce each potato with skewer in several places. Place potatoes, slightly apart, directly onto oven rack in moderate oven for 1 hour or until tender.

2 Remove from oven, cut potatoes in half, scoop out the flesh leaving a 1cm (½in) thick shell of potato.

3 Cook broccoli and carrot until tender, drain. Combine potato flesh, broccoli and carrot, mayonnaise and lemon juice. Fill potato halves with potato mixture.

4 Top with combined cheese and almonds. Sprinkle with paprika. Bake in moderate oven on oven tray for 15 minutes or until golden.

Serves 4

Glazed Pumpkin

Mushroom Salad

250g (½lb) button mushrooms

½ cup French dressing

2 tblspn light sour cream

1 clove garlic, crushed

2 tblspn chopped parsley

1 tblspn chopped chives

1 Wipe mushrooms with paper towel.

2 Trim stalks to within 1cm (½in) of cap.

3 Combine French dressing, sour cream, garlic, parsley and chives. Pour over mushrooms, mix well.

4 Cover, refrigerate overnight.

Serves 4

Glazed Pumpkin

½ butternut pumpkin

30g (1oz) butter

2 tblspn golden syrup

½ cup fresh wholemeal breadcrumbs

1 Cut pumpkins into 3cm (1¼in) slices, leaving skin on, but removing seeds.

2 Arrange pumpkin in greased shallow ovenproof dish. Bake covered with foil in moderate oven for 35 minutes.

3 Melt butter and golden syrup in pan, stir in breadcrumbs. Remove foil from dish. Pour mixture over pumpkin.

4 Bake, uncovered a further 20 minutes.

Serves 4

Orange Rice

1 cup brown rice

2 tspn grated orange rind

½ cup orange juice

2 tblspn chopped parsley

2 cups chicken stock

1 Place brown rice in saucepan, add remaining ingredients.

2 Bring to the boil, reduce heat, simmer, covered, for 40 minutes or until rice is tender and liquid is absorbed. Stir in extra chopped parsley, if desired.

Serves 4

Spiral Pasta with Spinach, Basil and Cheese

250g (½lb) spiral pasta

1 bunch spinach

1 tblspn olive oil

1 tblspn chopped fresh basil

¼ cup grated Parmesan cheese

1 Cook pasta in large pan boiling water for 10 minutes or until tender, drain.

2 Meanwhile wash spinach, drain, remove end stalks. Chop spinach leaves finely. Boil, steam or microwave spinach until just tender, drain. Add to drained pasta.

3 Add oil, basil and Parmesan cheese, toss well. Serve with extra Parmesan cheese, if desired.

Serves 4-6

Risotto with Cheese and Pinenuts

60g (2oz) butter or margarine

1 onion, finely chopped

2 cups brown rice

4 cups chicken stock

¼ cup pinenuts

¼ cup grated Parmesan cheese

1 Melt 40g (1½oz) of the butter in pan, cook onion until golden brown. Add rice, cook 3 minutes, stirring continually.

2 Add ½ cup stock. Stir the mixture continually, gradually adding more stock as it is absorbed.

3 Toast pinenuts on oven tray in moderate oven 5 minutes.

4 When the rice is cooked, remove from heat, add remaining butter cut into pieces, pinenuts and Parmesan cheese. Stir and serve.

Serves 4

Orange Rice; Spiral Pasta with Spinach, Basil and Cheese

Coleslaw

½ Chinese cabbage, finely shredded

1 carrot, grated

½ small red cabbage, finely shredded

1 cup bean shoots

2 bacon rashers, chopped

⅓ cup peanut oil

1 tblspn soy sauce

2 tspn sesame oil

2 tblspn rice vinegar (see note)

1 tblspn white vinegar

1 Combine vegetables in bowl.

2 Cook bacon until crisp, drain well. Add to salad.

3 Combine remaining ingredients in jar, shake well, pour over vegetables, mix well.

4 Cover, refrigerate for at least 2 hours before serving.

Note: rice vinegar is available from Asian food stores.

Serves 4

Carrots and Apples

3 large carrots, sliced

2 Granny Smith apples, peeled, cored and sliced

2 tblspn brown sugar

1 tspn grated lemon rind

¼ cup lemon juice

15g (½oz) butter

1 Boil, steam or microwave carrots until tender, drain.

2 Arrange half the carrots over base of greased casserole dish. Arrange apples over carrots. Sprinkle with brown sugar.

3 Arrange remaining carrot slices on top. Sprinkle with combined lemon rind and juice. Dot with butter.

4 Bake in moderate oven 45 minutes.

Serves 4-6

Cracked Wheat, Celery and Apple Salad

1 cup cracked wheat

2 sticks celery, sliced

1 Red Delicious apple, sliced

1 Granny Smith apple, sliced

¼ cup walnut halves

¼ cup light sour cream

1 tspn cider vinegar

1 tspn honey

pinch each cinnamon and nutmeg

1 Soak cracked wheat in plenty of water 1 hour, drain well.

2 Combine cracked wheat in salad bowl with celery, apples (leave skin on) and walnuts.

3 Combine remaining ingredients in screw-top jar, shake well, pour over salad, toss well.

Serves 4

Spinach with Water Chestnuts

1 bunch English spinach, washed and chopped

2 tblspn low salt soy sauce

2 tspn oil

½ tspn sesame oil

1 tblspn rice vinegar

¼ tspn sugar

1 227g (7oz) can whole water chestnuts, drained and halved

1 Combine soy sauce, oils, vinegar and sugar in pan.

2 Add wet spinach and water chestnuts. Bring to the boil, reduce heat, simmer 5 minutes, stirring occasionally. Serve immediately.

Serves 4

Cracked Wheat, Celery and Apple Salad

COOKING FOR PROBLEM EATERS

Allergies make eating a misery for some children and their parents. Here are a few recipes that will help avoid some of the more common allergic problems.

Milk Free Ice-Cream

1 cup non-dairy whitener

1 tspn gelatine

1 tspn water

1 tblspn sugar

½ cup warm water, extra

1 tspn vanilla essence.

1 Sprinkle gelatine over water, dissolve over hot water.

2 Combine whitener, dissolved gelatine and water, sugar, warm water and vanilla in bowl. Refrigerate until partially set (egg white consistency).

3 Beat with electric mixer until foamy, pour into container. Freeze until set.

Makes about 3 cups

Date and Walnut Cookies

1 egg

¾ cup brown sugar

¼ tspn baking powder

¼ cup soy bean flour

⅔ cup oat flour

¼ cup finely chopped walnuts

½ tspn vanilla essence

¼ cup chopped dates

¼ cup walnut pieces, for decoration

1 Cream together the egg and sugar. Add remaining ingredients, mix well.

2 Place teaspoonfuls of mixture onto a greased baking tray, press a piece of walnut into top of each biscuit.

3 Bake in moderate oven for 12-15 minutes.

Makes about 30

Banana Bread

1 cup brown sugar

90g (3oz) butter, softened

2 eggs

½ tspn baking soda

1½ cups rye flour

½ cup cornflour

pinch salt

½ tspn mixed spice

3 bananas, mashed

1 Beat sugar and butter together until creamy. Add eggs one at a time, beating well after each addition.

2 Add soda, flours, salt, spice and bananas; mix well.

3 Pour mixture into a greased loaf pan, bake in moderate oven 35-40 minutes. Stand on wire rack to cool, slice, spread with butter.

Makes 1 loaf

Fruit Slice

125g (4oz) margarine

½ cup brown sugar, firmly packed

½ cup rye flour

½ cup soya or buckwheat flour

2 tblspn cornflour

¼ tspn bicarbonate of soda

½ tspn cream of tartar

Carob Mousse

For children who cannot tolerate chocolate and egg yolk.

3 cups skim milk

¾ cup cornflour

2 tspn vanilla essence

¼ cup carob powder

4 tblspn boiling water

1 tblspn grated orange rind

1 tblspn orange juice

200g (6½oz) carton low-fat yoghurt

2 egg whites

strawberries

1 Place 2½ cups milk in a saucepan and bring to a mid-boil.

2 Add remaining half cup of milk to cornflour and mix to a smooth paste. Add vanilla essence.

3 Combine carob with boiling water, mix to a paste. Add orange rind and juice.

4 Combine cornflour mixture with carob mixture. Add this to the hot milk and stir over heat until sauce thickens. Remove from heat and fold in yoghurt.

5 Beat egg whites until stiff peaks form. Fold whites into mixture. Pour into serving glasses, refrigerate for at least two hours. Serve topped with fresh strawberries.

Serves 8

Above: Banana Bread; Date and Walnut Cookies. Inset: Carob Mousse

1 tspn salt

¼ tspn mixed spice

¼ cup water

1 egg, beaten

1 cup mixed fruit

1 Cream margarine and sugar until light and fluffy. Sift flours together with bicarbonate of soda, cream of tartar and salt and mixed spice. Add to creamed margarine and sugar mixture.

2 Add water, egg and mixed fruit, mix well.

3 Spread mixture in a greased 19cm x 29cm (7½ x 11in) lamington tin. Bake in moderately hot oven 30 minutes. Cut into squares while warm. Cool in tin.

Makes about 15

TEENAGERS IN THE FAMILY

When the children grow older, there's increased pressure on them to eat all sorts of junk food. You can help carry on the good work of earlier years by encouraging them to enjoy dishes that are healthy, different and fun.

THROWING A PARTY

Cheesy Capsicum (Pepper) Pizza with Thick Wholemeal Crust

WHOLEMEAL CRUST

2 cups wholemeal flour

2 cups plain flour

7g (¼oz) sachet dried yeast

1 tspn sugar

1 tspn salt

2 tblspn oil

1⅓ cups warm water

TOPPING

30g (1oz) butter

2 tblspn oil

2 onions, sliced

2 red capsicums (peppers), chopped

2 green capsicums (peppers), chopped

1 clove garlic, crushed

2 tspn dried oregano

⅓ cup tomato paste

2 tblspn dry white wine

4 cups grated mozzarella cheese

1 cup grated Parmesan cheese

1 To make crust, sift flours into bowl, add yeast, sugar and salt. Make a well in the centre, add combined oil and water, and mix to a firm dough. Turn onto a lightly floured surface and knead for 15 minutes.

2 Place dough in an oiled bowl, cover with a teatowel and stand in a warm place for half an hour. When dough has doubled in size, turn onto floured surface and knead for a further 5 minutes. Divide dough into two and roll each piece out to cover a greased 22cm (9in) pizza pan.

3 Melt butter and oil over medium heat in large frypan. Add onions capsicums, garlic and oregano, cook until tender.

4 Mix together tomato paste and wine, spread evenly over the bases. Sprinkle half the combined cheeses over the bases, then onion mixture, top with remaining cheese. Bake in moderate oven for 20-25 minutes or until base is cooked.

Makes 2

Cheesy Capsicum (Pepper) Pizza with Thick Wholemeal Crusts; Tacos with Salmon and Avocado

Cheesy Salmon Patties

Cheesy Salmon Patties

310g (10oz) can drained butter beans

210g (6½oz) can salmon

½ cup mashed potato

¾ cup grated cheddar cheese

¼ cup grated Parmesan cheese

1 small onion, grated

1 tblspn finely chopped chives

½ cup plain flour

2 tblspn lemon juice

1 egg, lightly beaten

1 cup stale wholemeal breadcrumbs

oil for deep frying

1 Mash butter beans to a paste. Drain salmon, remove skin and bones, add to beans.

2 Mix potato, cheeses, onion, chives, flour and lemon juice into salmon and beans. Add egg and mix well.

3 Divide mixture evenly into 6-8 portions, shape into patties. Toss each patty in breadcrumbs until totally covered.

4 Heat oil in a large frypan, add patties, pressing down with spatula to flatten. Cook 2 minutes each side until golden and cooked through.

Makes 6-8

Roast Grape Seasoned Chicken

1 size 15 chicken

60g (2oz) butter

1 onion, finely chopped

1 clove garlic, crushed

1 cup wholemeal breadcrumbs

1 cup seedless grapes

1 egg

¼ tspn dried sage

2 tblspn wholemeal plain flour

¼ cup dry white wine

¾ cup water

½ cup skim milk

1 tblspn chopped parsley

1 Heat butter in pan, cook onion 5 minutes; stirring occasionally, add garlic, stir 1 minute, remove from heat, stir in breadcrumbs, grapes, egg and sage.

2 Fill cavity of chicken with seasoning, secure opening with skewer or sew up with a heavy needle and thread.

3 Bake chicken on rack in baking dish in moderate oven 1 hour, or until chicken is tender.

4 Remove chicken, keep warm. Drain juices, leaving 1 tablespoon in dish. Add flour, stir over heat 1 minute. Gradually stir in wine, water and milk. Stir until sauce boils and thickens, add parsley. Serve with chicken.

Serves 4-6

Lamb and Tomato Curry

Lamb and Tomato Curry

4 lamb chump chops
2 tblspn butter
1 onion, roughly chopped
1 clove garlic, crushed
1 tblspn mild curry powder
1 tspn cumin powder
400g (13oz) can peeled tomatoes
1 apple, cored, peeled and chopped
2 tblspn sultanas
2 tblspn slivered almonds

1 Cut away flesh from chops, discard bones and excess fat, cut meat into 2cm (¾in) cubes.

2 Melt butter in a large saucepan, add onions and garlic; cook until tender.

3 Add curry powder and cumin, mix well. Add lamb and cook until browned on outside.

4 Add tomatoes and their juice, cook for 3 minutes. Add apple, sultanas and almonds; reduce heat and simmer 20 minutes. Serve with brown rice.

Serves 2

Rice Salad with Lemon Dressing

½ red capsicum (pepper)
2 cups cooked brown rice
4 diagonally sliced spring onions (scallions)
3-4 baby squash
¼ cup currants
¼ cup walnut pieces
2 tblspn chopped parsley
½ green apple, cut into cubes
½ red apple, cut into cubes
2 tblspn lemon juice
1 tblspn orange juice
1 tspn vinegar
1 tspn oil

1 Cut capsicum into small pieces discard seeds. Combine rice, spring onions, capsicum, squash, currants, walnuts and parsley in a large bowl.

2 Mix together lemon juice, orange juice, vinegar and oil, drop apple pieces into lemon dressing then mix apples and dressing into salad.

Serves 6

Spinach Pie

8 large spinach leaves (silverbeet)

30g (1oz) butter

6 spring onions (scallion), chopped

½ red capsicum (pepper), seeded and finely chopped

1 tblspn chopped parsley

¼ tspn ground nutmeg

155g (5oz) feta cheese, crumbled

¾ cup cottage cheese

2 tblspn wheatgerm

3 eggs, lightly beaten

8 sheets filo pastry

30g (1oz) butter, melted, extra

1 Chop spinach and place in a large saucepan with water to 2cm (¾in) deep. Cover, bring to boil, reduce heat, simmer 2 minutes. Strain spinach, cool to room temperature, squeeze out as much water as possible.

2 Heat butter in small frying pan. Add spring onions, capsicum and parsley, cook 3 minutes. Transfer mixture to large bowl, add spinach, nutmeg, feta cheese, crumbled cottage cheese, wheatgerm and eggs, mix well.

3 Grease a lamington pan. Brush each layer of filo with extra melted butter. Place four pieces on top of each other, make 2 piles.

4 Place 1 pile in base of pan, trim around edges. Pour spinach mixture into pan. Place the remaining pile of filo on top, roll edges down. Brush top with butter. Bake in moderate oven 40 minutes, cut into six square slices.

Serves 6

Rice Salad with Lemon Dressing; Spinach Pie

CAKES, COOKIES, BISCUITS AND SLICES

School's over and the kitchen door bursts open to reveal your "starving" children. That's when a well-stocked cake tin and biscuit jar will help you spread the smiles around.

CAKES

Orange and Sultana Cake

750g (1½lb) sultanas

1¾ cups boiling water

½ cup orange juice

3 eggs

1 tblspn grated orange rind

1 cup brown sugar, firmly packed

½ cup oil

1¾ cups wholemeal self-raising flour

1 cup plain flour

1 Combine sultanas, water and orange juice in a bowl, stand 1 hour.

2 Beat eggs, rind and sugar in small bowl with electric mixer until thick and creamy, gradually beat in oil.

3 Transfer mixture to large bowl, fold in sifted flours and sultana mixture.

4 Spread into a greased and paper-lined 20cm (8in) round cake tin. Bake in moderately slow oven 1½ hours, or until cooked when tested. Stand 10 minutes before turning onto wire rack to cool.

Makes 1

Chocolate Apple Cake

1 cup self-raising wholemeal flour

½ tspn bicarbonate of soda

¼ cup cocoa

½ cup brown sugar

2 cooking apples, peeled and finely grated

2 eggs, lightly beaten

⅓ cup chopped pecan nuts

½ cup oil

icing sugar

1 apple, for decoration

1 Sift flour, bicarbonate soda and cocoa together in a large bowl. Make a well in the centre, add sugar, apples, eggs, pecan nuts and oil; mix well.

2 Pour mixture into a greased and lined 20cm (8in) deep cake tin. Bake in moderate oven for 40 minutes or until cooked when tested.

3 Cool on wire rack, dust with sifted icing sugar and decorate with slices of apple.

Makes 1

Chocolate Apple Cake

Carrot and Zucchini Wholemeal Cake

2 eggs

1 cup raw sugar

⅓ cup sour cream

¾ cup grated zucchini

¾ cup grated carrot

½ cup oil

2 cups self-raising wholemeal flour

¼ tspn bicarbonate of soda

1 tspn mixed spice

CREAM CHEESE ICING

125g (4oz) packaged cream cheese

30g (1oz) butter, softened

1 tspn vanilla essence

1½ cups icing sugar

¼ cup finely chopped walnuts, to decorate

1 In a food processor, combine eggs, sugar, sour cream, zucchini and carrot until combined. While motor is running, pour oil through shute.

2 Sift flour, soda and spice into a large bowl; stir in zucchini mixture, mix well.

3 Pour into a greased deep 20cm (8in) cake pan; bake in moderate oven for 45 minutes, or until cooked when tested. Stand for 5 minutes, then turn onto wire rack to cool.

4 To make icing: Beat cream cheese, butter and essence with electric mixer until smooth, gradually beat in icing sugar, spread over cake, decorate with chopped walnuts.

Makes 1

Carrot and Zucchini (Courgette) Wholemeal Cake

Banana Cake with Maple Icing

CAKE

1 cup wholemeal self-raising flour

1 cup self-raising flour

125g (4oz) butter or margarine

¾ cup caster sugar

½ tspn vanilla essence

3 medium, very ripe bananas, peeled and roughly mashed

2 eggs

½ cup natural yoghurt

ICING

45g (1½oz) butter or margarine

¾ cup icing sugar, sifted

2 tspn maple syrup

extra sliced banana to decorate

1 Grease a 20 x 15cm (8 x 6in) loaf tin with melted butter or margarine and line the base with greased greaseproof paper. Sift the flour into a mixing bowl. Return husks to bowl. Beat the butter or margarine until soft, add the sugar, vanilla essence and bananas and continue beating until the mixture is light and fluffy. Add 2 tablespoons of the flour and beat until well combined. Add the eggs one at a time, beating well after each addition.

2 Gently fold the remaining flour into the creamed mixture alternately with the yoghurt. Spoon cake mixture into the prepared tin and smooth the top level.

3 Bake at 180ºC (350ºF) for 1 hour or until golden brown and firm. Cool in the tin for 5 minutes, then turn out onto a wire rack and allow to cool completely.

4 To make icing: Beat butter or margarine in a small bowl until soft and creamy, add icing sugar and maple syrup and continue beating until mixture is smooth. Spread over cooled banana cake and decorate with sliced banana.

Makes 1

Date and Pecan Loaf

90g (3oz) butter, softened

1 cup brown sugar, firmly packed

1 cup chopped dates

¾ cup chopped pecans

1 cup boiling water

1¾ cups self-raising wholemeal flour

1 tspn mixed spice

1 tspn ground ginger

1 In a large bowl, combine butter, sugar, dates and pecans. Add water, stir until butter has melted; fold in remaining ingredients, mix well.

2 Spoon mixture into a greased and lined 23 x 13cm (9 x 5in) loaf pan and bake in moderate oven for 45 minutes, or until cooked when tested with a skewer. Serve sliced with butter.

Makes 1

Wholemeal Apricot and Coconut Loaf

1 cup coconut

1½ cups finely chopped dried apricots

1 cup hot milk

¼ cup honey

1 egg, lightly beaten

¾ cup wholemeal self-raising flour

¼ cup ground almonds

2 tblspn lemon juice

2 tblspn sugar

1 Toast coconut on a baking tray in oven for 5 minutes or until golden.

2 In a large bowl combine apricots, milk and honey, cover and stand for 1 hour. Stir egg, flour, almonds and ¾ cup coconut into apricot, milk and honey mixture; mix well.

3 Pour mixture into a greased and lined 14cm x 21cm (5½ x 8½in) loaf pan. Cook in moderate oven for about 45 minutes. Stand cake 5 minutes in pan. Turn onto wire rack.

4 Combine lemon juice and sugar over low heat until sugar has dissolved. Brush over top of cake while warm, sprinkle with extra toasted coconut.

Makes 1

Coffee and Walnut Cake

1 tblspn instant coffee

1 tblspn boiling water

125g (4oz) butter

⅞ cup caster sugar

2 eggs

1 tspn vanilla essence

1 cup self-raising flour

1 cup wholemeal self-raising flour

⅓ cup milk

60g (2oz) walnuts, chopped

1 Dissolve instant coffee in boiling water and set aside to cool. Grease a deep 20cm (8in) round cake tin and set oven at moderate, 180ºC (350ºF).

2 Cream butter, add sugar and beat until light. Add eggs one at a time and beat in well. Add vanilla essence. Fold in sifted flour alternately with coffee, milk and chopped walnuts. The mixture should be fairly soft.

3 Spoon into prepared tin and bake in preheated oven for 50-60 minutes.

Serves 8-10

Date and Pecan Loaf; Wholemeal Apricot and Coconut Loaf

Pumpkin Nut Slice

185g (6oz) butter or margarine

1 cup caster sugar

1 cup wholemeal plain flour

1 tspn bicarbonate of soda

½ tspn baking powder

½ tspn salt

1½ tspn cinnamon

½ tspn allspice

2 eggs, lightly beaten

½ cup chopped pecan nuts or walnuts

½ tspn vanilla essence

½ cup chopped raisins

1 cup drained, crushed pineapple

¾ cup cooked, mashed pumpkin

ICING

1½ cups sifted icing sugar

250g (½lb) softened cream cheese

½ tspn vanilla essence

2 tspn lemon juice

1 Grease and line the base of a 28 x 18cm (11 x 7in) deep lamington tin. Beat the butter or margarine until soft. Add sugar and beat until mixture is light and fluffy.

2 Sift all dry ingredients together, return husks to bowl, and add to the creamed mixture alternately with the beaten eggs. Stir in the nuts, vanilla essence, raisins, pineapple and pumpkin. Mix well and pour into the tin.

3 Bake at 180ºC (350ºF) for 1 hour, or until skewer inserted in the centre of the cake comes out clean. Cool on a wire rack. Spread icing over cake and decorate with pecan nuts.

4 To make icing: Place all the ingredients in a mixing bowl and beat until well combined, then increase speed until light and fluffy.

Makes 1

Muesli Slice

Carob Oat Bars

BISCUITS AND SLICES

Muesli Slice

125g (4oz) butter

2 tblspn honey

½ cup brown sugar

1 cup natural muesli

½ cup coconut

½ cup wholemeal flour

½ cup flaked almonds

½ cup currants

½ cup dried apricots, chopped

2 eggs, lightly beaten

1 Melt butter and honey together in a large saucepan; remove from heat. Stir in the sugar, muesli, coconut, flour, almonds, currants and apricots; mix well.

2 Add eggs and combine well. Press mixture into a greased and lined 19cm x 29cm (7½ x 11½in) lamington tin.

3 Bake in moderately slow oven for 30 minutes. Cool and then slice into squares.

Makes about 35

Carob Oat Bars

1 cup rolled oats

1 cup wholemeal flour

½ cup dark brown sugar

½ cup chopped hazelnuts

½ cup chopped carob

125g (4oz) butter, melted

3 tblspn honey

1 Combine all ingredients in a bowl, mix well.

2 Press the mixture into a greased and lined 19cm x 29cm (7½ x 11½in) lamington tin. Bake in moderate oven for about 25 minutes. Cool, and slice into bars.

Makes about 20 bars

Oat Bran Biscuits

1 cup wholemeal self-raising flour

2 tblspn custard powder

⅓ cup brown sugar

½ cup rolled oats

¼ cup unprocessed bran

150g (5oz) butter, chopped

2 tblspn honey

½ cup wheatgerm

1 Sift flour and custard powder into a bowl. Add sugar, oats and bran; mix well. Rub in butter; mix in the honey.

2 Roll teaspoonfuls of the mixture into balls and roll each in the wheatgerm.

3 Place biscuits on a greased oven tray leaving 3cm(1¼in) between each biscuit. Press each biscuit with a fork; bake in moderate oven 15 minutes.

Makes about 25

Fudge Peanut Delights

60g (2oz) butter

½ cup brown sugar

½ cup evaporated milk

125g (4oz) white chocolate, chopped

½ cup crunchy peanut butter

2 cups rolled oats

1 cup coconut

15 glace cherries

1 In a large saucepan, melt butter without boiling. Add sugar and milk, stir constantly without boiling until sugar has dissolved; then boil for 3 minutes, stirring occasionally.

2 Add chocolate and peanut butter, stir until chocolate has melted; remove from heat then add oats and coconut and mix well.

3 Drop teaspoon full of mixture into paper patty cases. Top each one with ½ glace cherry; refrigerate for an hour, or until set.

Makes about 30

Wholemeal Apricot Slice

1½ cups wholemeal plain flour

1 cup wholemeal self-raising flour

125g (4oz) butter

¼ cup milk

1 egg, lightly beaten

1 tblspn honey

1 cup chopped dried apricots

1 cup water

2 tspn grated orange rind

1 tblspn orange juice

1 egg white

1 tblspn sugar

1 Combine sifted flours in large bowl, return husks to bowl. Rub in butter. Stir in combined milk, egg and honey.

2 Knead dough on a lightly floured surface until smooth.

3 Roll out half the pastry to line base of a greased 19cm x 29cm (7½ x 11in) lamington tin.

4 Combine apricots, water, orange rind and juice in a saucepan, bring to the boil, reduce heat, simmer uncovered for 10 minutes or until liquid has evaporated; stir occasionally. Cool to room temperature.

5 Spread filling evenly over pastry. Roll out remaining pastry to cover filling. Brush lightly with egg white, sprinkle with sugar. Bake in moderately hot oven for 10 minutes, reduce heat to moderate, bake for 20 minutes. Cool in tin, cut when cold.

Makes about 15 squares

Oat Bran Biscuits; Fudge Peanut Delights

Pineapple Smoothie

200g (6½oz) carton plain yoghurt

450g (14oz) can crushed pineapple

½ cup vanilla ice-cream

1 Puree all ingredients in blender or processor, pour into glasses.

Serves 4

Watermelon Fizz

½ cup watermelon flesh

½ cup soda water

crushed ice

1 Remove pips from watermelon. In a processor, blend ice and watermelon for 30 seconds. Pour into glass, top with soda water.

Serves 1

Orange Honey Whip

2 cups orange juice

4 oranges, peeled and chopped

2 tblspn low-fat natural yoghurt

2 tblspn honey

1 Combine all ingredients in a food processor; blend until smooth. Serve chilled.

Serves 2

Orange Honey Whip; Mango Milkshake

DRINKS

Orange Punch

1 red apple

1 green apple

5 cups orange juice

juice of a lemon

2 tblspn honey

1 thick slice watermelon

1 Cut each apple into chucks, discard cores. Pour orange juice into a large jug, add apple pieces.

2 Heat lemon juice and honey over low heat until honey has melted. Leave to cool, stir into orange juice.

3 Remove skin from watermelon, cut into cubes or scoop into balls with a melon scooper; drop into orange juice; chill, pour into tall glasses.

Serves 6

Mango Milkshake

1 mango

1 cup crushed ice

1 cup milk

1 Remove skin from mango, cut flesh away from stone.

2 Place mango, ice and milk in blender or processor, blend until smooth.

3 Serve in tall glasses, decorate with a strawberry.

Makes 2

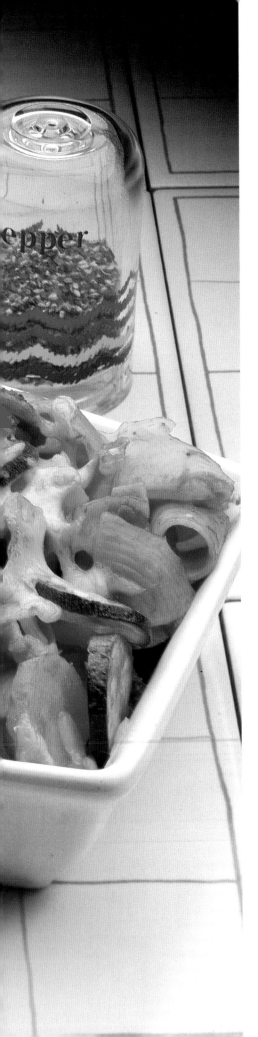

Pasta, Rice And Beans

Not only convenient to store and quick to prepare, these ingredients so often provide essential fibre for your family's diet. Try these dishes, you'll find they become regular favourites.

Vegeroni Vegetable Bake with Cheese

250g (1lb) packet vegeroni
1 tblspn oil
1 onion, chopped
1 carrot, chopped
1 stick celery, chopped
1 zucchini, chopped
1 cup broccoli flowerets
400g (13oz) tomatoes, undrained
¼ cup tomato paste
2 tblspn dry white wine
1 clove garlic, crushed
250g (½lb) grated mozzarella cheese

1 Cook vegeroni in large pot of boiling water until tender, drain, pour into base of shallow ovenproof dish.

2 Heat oil in pan, cook onion, carrot and celery 10 minutes; stirring occasionally.

3 Add zucchini, broccoli, tomatoes, tomato paste, wine and garlic. Cook, stirring occasionally, 20 minutes. Add a little water from time to time to keep it moist. Mixture should not be dry.

4 Add vegetable mixture to vegeroni, mix well. Sprinkle with grated cheese. Bake in moderate oven 10 minutes or until cheese melts and vegeroni heated through. Serve with salad.

Serves 4-6

Vegeroni Vegetable Bake with Cheese

Oriental Noodles

1kg (2lb) fresh rice noodles (see note)
1 tblspn oil
2 onions, sliced
125g (4oz) bacon, chopped
2 tblspn dry sherry
1 clove garlic, crushed
2 cups bean sprouts, firmly packed
2 sticks celery, chopped
4 spring onions (scallions), chopped
1 tblspn oil, extra
2 tblspn light soy sauce
2 tblspn dark soy sauce

1 Cut noodles into thin strips.

2 Heat oil in pan, add onions and bacon, stir-fry until onions are lightly browned.

3 Add sherry and garlic, stir-fry 1 minute. Add bean sprouts, celery and spring onions, stir-fry until vegetables are just tender, remove from pan.

4 Heat extra oil in pan, add noodles, stir gently until heated through, add soy sauces and vegetable mixture, stir-fry until heated through. Serve with green salad.

Note: Fresh rice noodles can be obtained from Asian food stores.

Serves 6

Spinach and Cheese Lasagna

250g (½lb) spinach, washed and finely chopped

500g (1lb) ricotta cheese

125g (4oz) mozzarella cheese, grated

250g (½lb) spinach, washed and finely chopped

2 spring onions (scallions), chopped

1 tspn dried basil

1 tspn dried oregano

⅓ cup chopped parsley

1 tblspn oil

1 onion, chopped

1 carrot, chopped

1 stick celery, chopped

1 clove garlic, crushed

1 tspn dried basil

1 bay leaf

½ cup white wine

800g (26oz) can peeled tomatoes, undrained and mashed

2 tblspn tomato paste

½ cup unsweetened apple puree

3 tblspn grated Parmesan cheese

6 instant lasagna sheets

1 Boil, steam or microwave spinach until wilted, drain well.

2 Mix together in a bowl the spinach, ricotta, mozzarella, spring onions, basil, oregano and parsley, mix well.

3 Heat oil in pan, cook onion, carrot and celery 2 minutes, add garlic, cook 1 minute.

4 Stir in basil, bay leaf and wine, bring to the boil, boil 3 minutes. Add tomatoes, tomato paste and apple puree. Bring to boil, reduce heat, simmer 30 minutes. Remove bay leaf. Puree sauce in processor or blender until smooth.

5 Stir in Parmesan cheese.

6 Assemble lasagna by placing a third of the tomato mixture on base of 28 x 33cm (11 x 13in) baking dish.

7 Place 3 sheets of lasagna in single layer over sauce, spread half the ricotta cheese mixture over lasagna. Top with a third of the tomato mixture.

8 Place remaining 3 sheets of lasagna over sauce, spread remaining half of ricotta mixture over lasagna. Top with remaining tomato mixture.

9 Cover with foil. Bake lasagna in moderate oven 20 minutes, remove foil, bake further 20 minutes. Serve with a green salad. Sprinkle with extra Parmesan cheese if desired.

Serves 4-6

Brown Fried Rice

1¼ cup brown rice

2 tspn oil

3 eggs, beaten

½ tspn sesame oil

1 tblspn oil, extra

2 tspn grated fresh ginger

250g (½lb) Chinese barbecued pork, finely chopped (see note)

4 spring onions (scallions), chopped

500g (1lb) cooked prawns (shrimp), shelled

1 small lettuce, shredded

1 tblspn light soy sauce

1 Cook rice in large pot of boiling water 25 minutes or until tender, rinse under cold water, drain well.

2 Heat 1 teaspoon oil in pan, pour in half the combined egg and sesame oil mixture, when set, turn, cook other side, remove from pan. Repeat with remaining oil and egg mixture. Roll up omelette, slice into thin strips.

3 Heat extra oil in wok, add rice and ginger, stir-fry 3 minutes.

4 Add pork, spring onions, prawns, lettuce and omelette strips, stir-fry few minutes, add soy sauce, serve immediately with steamed or stir-fried vegetables.

Note: Chinese barbecued pork is available from Asian food stores.

Serves 4

Spaghetti with Meat Sauce

Use the best lean mince to make a healthier low fat meat sauce.

250g (½lb) spaghetti
1 tblspn oil
1 onion, finely chopped
1 clove garlic, crushed
500g (1lb) lean beef mince
2 x 400g (13oz) cans tomatoes, undrained
¼ cup tomato paste
¼ cup dry white wine
½ tspn dried oregano
½ tspn dried basil
1 cup beef stock
Parmesan cheese for garnish

1 Heat oil in pan, cook onion 5 minutes, stirring occasionally, add garlic, cook 1 minute. Remove onion and garlic mixture from pan.

2 Cook mince in batches in hot pan, stirring continually until lightly browned and cooked through.

3 Puree tomatoes in blender or processor until smooth.

4 Return all mince to pan with onion mixture and remaining ingredients. Being to the boil, reduce heat, simmer 30 minutes.

5 Cook spaghetti in large pot of boiling water 12 minutes or until just tender, drain. Serve spaghetti with meat sauce and grated Parmesan cheese if desired. Serve with salad.

Serves 4-6

Spinach and Cheese Lasagna

Paella

30g (1oz) butter

1 onion, finely chopped

⅔ cup brown rice

2 cups chicken stock

1 cup cooked chopped chicken

1 cup chopped ham

1 cup cooked prawns (shrimp), shelled and chopped

2 tblspn lemon juice

2 tblspn chopped parsley

1 Heat butter in large, shallow pan, cook onion 5 minutes; stirring occasionally.

2 Add rice, cook, stirring 2 minutes. Add stock, bring to boil, reduce heat, simmer, covered 40 minutes or until rice is tender.

3 Add chicken, ham, prawns and lemon juice, mix well. Cook until heated through. Serve sprinkled with parsley. Serve with salad.

Serves 4-6

Rice with Prawns (Shrimp)

1½ cups brown rice

pinch saffron

500g (1lb) cooked prawns (shrimp)

2 tspn oil

3 spring onions (scallion), finely chopped

1 red capsicum (pepper), finely chopped

1 green capsicum (pepper), finely chopped

1 tblspn chopped chives

¼ cup bottled French dressing

½ tspn curry powder

¼ tspn cumin

1 Cook rice with saffron in large pot of boiling water 30 minutes. Drain, keep warm.

2 Shell and devein prawns, chop into large pieces. Heat oil in pan, add spring onions and capsicums, cook few minutes or until heated through.

3 Add prawns, cook until just heated through.

4 Add prawn mixture to rice, toss well. Combine chives, dressing, curry and cumin, add to rice and prawn mixture. Toss through, serve hot or cold with a green salad or coleslaw.

Serves 4

Macaroni and Cauliflower Cheese

250g (½lb) wholemeal macaroni

1 small cauliflower, cut into flowerets

30g (1oz) butter

2 tblspn wholemeal plain flour

1 cup milk

125g (4oz) grated cheese

1 tblspn wheatgerm

1 Cook macaroni in large pot of boiling water 12 minutes or until tender, drain well.

2 Boil, steam or microwave cauliflower flowerets until just tender, drain.

3 Combine macaroni and cauliflower in shallow ovenproof dish.

4 Heat butter in pan, add flour, cook, stirring, 1 minute. Stir in milk, cook until sauce boils and thickens.

5 Pour the sauce over macaroni and cauliflower mixture, mix to combine. Sprinkle with cheese and wheatgerm. Bake in moderately hot oven 15 minutes.

Serves 4-6

Ravioli with Tomato Sauce

250g (½lb) fresh or frozen ravioli (see note)

1 small onion, chopped

800g (1½lb) peeled tomatoes, undrained

3 carrots, chopped

1 clove garlic, crushed

¼ cup light sour cream

1 tblspn grated Parmesan cheese

Paella

1 Cook ravioli in large pot of boiling water 20 minutes or until tender.

2 Combine onion, tomatoes, carrots and garlic in saucepan. Bring to the boil, reduce heat, simmer 20 minutes.

3 Puree mixture in processor or blender until smooth. Return mixture to saucepan, stir in sour cream. Reheat without boiling.

4 Place hot ravioli into individual dishes then pour warmed sauce over. Serve sprinkled with Parmesan cheese.

Note: Buy fresh ravioli at a pasta shop or frozen at the supermarket.

Serves 4

Brown Rice and Corn Loaf

1½ cups brown rice.

15g (½oz) butter

3 sticks celery, finely chopped

1 onion, finely chopped

2 tspn French mustard

2 tblspn wholemeal plain flour

½ cup milk

310g (10oz) can corn kernels, drained

2 tblspn chopped parsley

2 eggs, beaten

½ cup grated cheese

1 Cook rice in boiling water 30 minutes or until tender, drain well.

2 Heat butter in pan, cook celery and onion 5 minutes, stirring occasionally.

3 Add mustard and flour, cook, stirring 1 minute. Add milk, cook, stirring until sauce boils and thickens.

4 Add rice, corn, parsley and eggs, mix well.

5 Line a greased 23 x 12cm (9 x 5in) loaf tin with aluminium foil. Spread rice mixture into tin, sprinkle top with grated cheese. Bake, uncovered in moderate oven 40 minutes or until set and golden brown. Serve with salad.

Serves 4-6

Tofu and Rice Stir-fry

3 cups cooked brown rice

1 tblspn oil

1 onion, chopped

1 carrot, chopped

1 stick celery, chopped

½ cup cauliflower flowerets

125g (4oz) tofu, chopped

1 tblspn tamari (see note)

1 Heat oil in pan, cook onion 5 minutes, stirring occasionally.

2 Add remaining vegetables, cook 5 minutes.

3 Add tofu, mix well, cook 3 minutes.

4 Add tamari and rice, cook gently until heated through.

Note: Tamari is available from health food shops. If unavailable, substitute with soy sauce.

Serves 4

Bean Burgers

1 red capsicum (pepper), finely chopped

1 cup mashed potato

310g (10oz) can butter beans (cannellini style) drained and mashed

½ cup wholemeal breadcrumbs

1 tblspn sesame seeds

1 egg, beaten

2 tblspn milk

extra breadcrumbs

oil

1 Combine capsicum, potato, beans, breadcrumbs and sesame seeds. Shape into patties.

2 Dip into combined egg and milk then toss in breadcrumbs.

3 Brush both sides with oil, place on oven tray, bake in moderate oven 30 minutes. Turn half way through cooking time.

Serves 2-4

Capsicums (Peppers) with Bean Filling

4 red or green capsicums (peppers)

BEAN FILLING

2 tblspn olive oil

1 onion, chopped

2 tblspn ground cumin

1 clove garlic, crushed

¼ cup tomato paste

¼ cup chicken stock

400g (13oz) can tomatoes, undrained, crushed

400g (13oz) can red kidney beans, drained

1 Cut capsicums lengthwise in half, scoop out seeds.

2 Heat oil in a saucepan, add onion, stir-fry until tender.

3 Add remaining ingredients, bring to the boil, reduce heat, simmer uncovered for 10 minutes or until mixture has reduced and thickened.

4 Spoon bean filling into capsicum shells, place onto a baking tray. Bake in moderate oven for 20 minutes or until heated through and capsicum is tender.

Serves 4

Chilli Con Carne Beans

3 tblspn water

2 onions, chopped

2 cloves garlic, crushed

1 large red capsicum (pepper), chopped

2 x 425g (13½oz) cans red kidney beans, drained

2 large carrots, sliced

250g (½lb) green beans, cut into 3cm lengths

2 x 400g (13oz) cans tomatoes, undrained, crushed

1 can tomato juice

¼ tspn chilli powder

⅓ cup chopped parsley

Capsicums (Peppers) with Bean Filling; Chilli Con Carne Beans

1 Heat water in a saucepan, add onion and garlic, stir over heat until onion is tender.

2 Add remaining ingredients, bring to boil, reduce heat and simmer uncovered until reduced and thickened. Serve with rice or pasta.

Serves 6

Minestrone Casserole

1 tblspn oil

1 onion, chopped

1 carrot, chopped

1 stick celery, chopped

1 clove garlic, crushed

1 zucchini (courgette), chopped

1 potato, chopped

½ cup chopped green beans

½ cup chopped mushrooms

800g (26oz) can peeled tomatoes

½ tspn dried basil

½ tspn dried oregano

2 cups chicken stock

1 tblspn cornflour

1 tblspn water

2 x 310g (10oz) cans red kidney beans, drained

¼ cup chopped fresh parsley

2 tblspn chopped fresh chives

1 Heat oil in flameproof casserole dish. Cook onion, carrot and celery over medium heat for 10 minutes; stirring occasionally.

2 Add garlic, zucchini, potato, beans and mushrooms, cook further 5 minutes.

3 Add tomatoes, breaking them up using the back of a wooden spoon. Add basil, oregano and stock, cover, bake in moderate oven 45 minutes.

4 Add combined cornflour and water, place over medium heat, cook until mixture boils and thickens. Add beans, parsley and chives, re-heat before serving with wholemeal noodles or toast.

Serves 4

GIFTS, FETES AND SPECIAL OCCASIONS

It's nice to be able to say you made a kitchen gift yourself, whether for a school fete or as a present for the teacher. These special occasion ideas will do you and your children proud.

Cashew Nut Cookies

125g (4oz) butter

⅓ cup caster sugar

1 tspn vanilla essence

1 egg yolk

1 cup plain flour, sifted

½ cup self-raising flour, sifted

2 tblspn wheatgerm

60g (2oz) roasted, unsalted cashews

1 Cream butter and sugar together until light and fluffy. Add vanilla and egg yolk, mix well.

2 Fold in flours, wheatgerm and mix to a firm dough. Roll into a sausage shape and wrap in grease-proof paper. Place in refrigerator for 30 minutes or until firm.

3 Slice dough into 6mm (¼in) slices and place on a greased baking tray. Press a cashew into each biscuit and bake in a moderate oven for 10-12 minutes or until beginning to turn golden in colour.

Makes about 4 dozen

Chocolate Almond Truffles

¼ cup almonds, finely chopped

½ cup thickened cream

125g (4oz) dark chocolate, chopped

15g (½oz) butter

¾ cup Rice Bubbles, finely chopped

1 Toast the almonds on a baking tray until just beginning to turn golden, about 5 minutes.

2 Place the cream and chocolate in a medium saucepan and stir over low heat until chocolate is melted. Cool slightly and stir in butter. Refrigerate until mixture is cool.

3 Beat mixture with electric mixer until soft peaks form. Return to refrigerator again until firm.

4 Shape teaspoonfuls of mixture into balls, roll in combined almonds and rice bubbles.

Makes about 24

Cashew Nut Cookies; Chocolate Almond Truffles

Quick Orange Jam

4 large oranges

4 cups water

3 cups sugar, approximately

1 tblspn rum

1 Peel oranges to remove all white pith, discard skins. Chop flesh roughly, discard seeds.

2 Place chopped flesh in large pan with water, cover, bring to boil, reduce heat, simmer 20 minutes or until just tender.

3 Measure orange mixture. Add ¾ cup sugar to each 1 cup of mixture.

4 Stir orange and sugar mixture in large pan over heat without boiling until sugar dissolves.

5 Boil rapidly, uncovered, without stirring for 20 minutes or until jam will jell when tested on a cold saucer.

6 Stand 5 minutes, stir in rum, pour into hot sterilised jars, seal when cold.

Makes about 3 cups

Chocolate Surprises

200g (6½oz) cooking chocolate, chopped

200g (6½oz) milk chocolate, chopped

15g (½oz) copha

dried apricots

unsalted peanuts

50 coloured foil containers

1 Combine chocolates and copha in bowl. Stand over hot water, stir occasionally until melted.

2 Place a small amount of chopped apricots or peanuts in base of the foil containers.

3 Pour chocolate mixture into jug with a narrow spout. Pour chocolate in a thin stream into containers until tops are level.

4 Decorate tops of chocolates with corresponding apricot or peanut. Refrigerate or store in a cool, dry place until set.

5 Package chocolates for sale in small clear plastic boxes lined with colourful tissue paper.

Makes about 50

Festive Almond Fruit Cake

150g (5oz) apricots, cut in quarters

150g (5oz) red glace cherries

150g (5oz) green glace cherries

½ cup raisins

1½ cups brazil nuts

½ cup stoneless prunes

1 cup pecans

1 cup packaged ground almonds

½ tspn baking powder

3 eggs

2 tblspn honey

2 tspn vanilla essence

1 Combine all fruit and nuts in large bowl, stir in the ground almonds and baking powder.

2 Beat eggs until thick and creamy with electric mixer, beat in honey and vanilla essence. Pour egg mixture into fruit mixture.

3 Spread mixture into 2 small greased and lined loaf pans, pressing mixture firmly down into pans. Bake in slow oven for 1½ hours. Cool cakes in pans.

Makes 2 cakes

Festive Almond Fruit Cake

Left: Apricot Fruit Ring Cake. Above: Wholemeal Shortbread

Wholemeal Shortbread

250g (½lb) butter

½ cup brown sugar

1 cup wholemeal plain flour, sifted

1 cup plain flour, sifted

¼ cup rice flour

¼ cup wheatgerm

1 Beat butter and sugar together with electric mixer until light and fluffy. Stir in combined dry ingredients in two lots to make a firm dough.

2 Turn dough onto floured surface and lightly knead until smooth, about 2 minutes.

3 Roll out dough to about a 1cm (½in) thickness, and cut into a 20cm (8in) round. Use thumb and forefinger of one hand and forefinger of the other to pinch edge of shortbread decoratively, if desired.

4 Mark shortbread into 8 equal slices, being careful not to cut right through. Bake in moderately slow oven for 30-40 minutes or until beginning to brown.

Makes 1

Apricot Fruit Ring Cake

185g (6oz) butter

½ cup caster sugar

3 eggs

¾ cup plain flour

2 tspn mixed spice

500g (1lb) dried apricots, chopped

125g (4oz) glace apricots, chopped

250g (½lb) currants

250g (½lb) pecan nuts, chopped

TOPPING

15-20 dried apricots

¼ cup apricot jam

2 tblspn brandy

20 pecan nuts

1 Beat butter and sugar together until light and fluffy. Add eggs one at a time. Stir in flour and spice, then add fruit and pecans, mix well.

2 Press mixture firmly into a well-greased and lined 20cm (8in) ring tin. Bake in a slow oven for 1½ hours, or until cake has slightly shrunk away from side of tin. Cool in tin.

3 To make topping: Soak apricots in warm water for 15 minutes, drain and dry with absorbent paper. In a small saucepan heat jam and brandy, remove just before boiling.

4 Brush top of cold cake with half jam mixture. Arrange apricots and nuts decoratively on top of cake and brush remaining jam mixture over top.

Makes 1 cake

Orange Passionfruit Butter

4 eggs, lightly beaten

½ cup caster sugar

¼ cup orange juice

¼ cup lime juice

¼ cup passionfruit pulp

125g (4oz) unsalted butter, chopped

1 Whisk the eggs and sugar together in the top of a double saucepan, whisk in juices, passionfruit pulp and butter.

2 Using a wooden spoon stir mixture constantly over simmering water until mixture thickens and coats the back of a spoon.

3 Pour mixture into hot, sterilised jar, about 2 cup capacity, and seal when cool.

Makes about 2 cups

Walnut Crunchies

125g (4oz) butter

⅔ cup raw sugar

2 tblspn golden syrup

1 egg, lightly beaten

1 cup dessicated coconut

1½ cups wholemeal self-raising flour

1 cup walnuts

1 Melt butter in saucepan, stir in sugar, golden syrup and egg, then coconut and flour.

2 Use hands to form balls (teaspoonfuls). Place onto greased oven trays, spaced 3cm (1¼ in) apart to allow spreading.

3 Press walnut halves on top. Flatten biscuits slightly. Bake in slow oven 30 minutes or until golden. Cool on wire rack.

Makes about 18

Sesame Caramels

¾ cup sesame seeds

1 cup brown sugar

90g (3oz) butter

2 tblspn honey

⅓ cup liquid glucose

½ cup sweetened condensed milk

¼ cup sunflower seeds, chopped

1 Place sesame seeds in frypan and stir over a low heat until seeds are golden. Remove from pan to cool.

2 In a large saucepan, combine sugar, butter, honey, glucose and condensed milk, stir over low heat until sugar is dissolved, but not boiling. Slowly bring to the boil and cook uncovered for 7 minutes, stirring constantly.

3 Stir in ¼ cup of the toasted sesame seeds and the sunflower seeds. Pour mixture into a foil-lined 29 x 19cm (11½ x 7½in) lamington tin. Cool to room temperature.

4 Cut caramel into 4 strips lengthwise; fold each strip in half and roll into a log shape about 2cm (¾in) diameter. Roll each log in the remaining sesame seeds, refrigerate until ready to cut into slices.

Makes about 60

Orange Passionfruit Butter;
Sesame Caramels

WHEN FOOD CAN BE FUN

Parties, barbecues, holidays, all are occasions for something different to eat. In the following pages you'll find dozens of good suggestions, plus enjoyable drinks and a special section of recipes for children to cook themselves.

A PARTY FOR 10

Pikelet Faces

1 cup wholemeal self-raising flour

1 cup white self-raising flour

⅔ cup milk

2 tspn grated orange rind

2 tblspn orange juice

3 tblspn oil

30g (1oz) butter, melted

1 tblspn cocoa

extra butter, for pan

HONEY BUTTER

2 tblspn honey

60g (2oz) softened butter

1 Sift flours into bowl, make a well in the centre, add combined milk, orange rind, orange juice, oil and butter. Using wooden spoon, stir until smooth (or place mixture in processor for 1 minute).

2 Place half cup of the mixture into another bowl and add the cocoa and stir until smooth. Spoon cocoa mixtue into a piping bag, fitted with a plain tube.

3 Heat extra butter in pan. Pipe eyes and mouth on to pan and leave to cook for 30 seconds. Gently pour a tablespoon of orange pikelet mixture on top of the face and turn pikelet over when bubbles begin to appear.

4 Lightly cook other side and remove from pan. Serve with the honey butter.

5 To make Honey Butter: Stir honey into butter until combined.

Makes about 20

Sausage Bread Rolls

10 slices wholemeal bread

¼ cup tomato sauce

5 thin chicken sausages, grilled

5 rashers bacon

30g (1oz) butter, melted

1 Using a sharp knife remove crusts from bread. Spread each slice with the tomato sauce.

2 Cut each sausage in half and place diagonally in centre of each slice of bread; roll up.

3 Cut each rasher of bacon in half lengthwise and roll each piece of bacon around the centre of the rolls.

4 Brush the bread with the butter and place on a baking tray. Bake for 15 minutes in moderate oven or until golden.

Makes 10

Sausage Bread Rolls; Pikelet Faces

Party Sandwiches

2 loaves wholemeal bread

butter or margarine

fish paste

⅓ cup cream cheese

1 tblspn chopped parsley

2 hard-boiled eggs, mashed

2 tspn mayonnaise

peanut butter

Vegemite

1 Butter bread.

2 Make 4 sandwiches using either fish paste, combined cream cheese and parsley, combined egg and mayonnaise, peanut butter or Vegemite.

3 Remove crusts. Cut each sandwich into 3 fingers or 4 triangles. Arrange on a tray, decorated with sprigs of parsley.

*Makes 20 sandwiches
or 60 fingers or 80 triangles*

Note: Sandwiches may be frozen in batches of 3 or 4, wrapped securely in plastic wrap. Remove from freezer 2 hours before serving. When almost thawed, cut into fingers or triangles and cover tray with a damp teatowel to prevent sandwiches drying out.

Wheatmeal Faces

1 packet wheatmeal biscuits

250g (½lb) packet cream cheese

1 tspn grated lemon rind

Smarties

jelly beans

1 Beat cream cheese in processor or electric mixer with lemon rind and sugar until smooth. Spread flat side of biscuits with cream cheese mixture.

2 Press 2 smarties and a jelly bean into cream cheese side to make a face. Allow to set for 30 minutes before serving. Faces may be made up to 2 hours in advance.

Makes about 25

Banana Clock Cake

250g (½lb) butter, softened

1 cup brown sugar, firmly packed

4 eggs

2 cups mashed banana

1 cup sour cream

½ cup oil

4 cups self-raising flour, sifted

1 tblspn mixed spice

ICING

250g (½lb) butter, softened

500g (1lb) icing sugar

1 tblspn milk

food colours

DECORATIONS

1 cup coconut, coloured if desired

licorice, soft

Smarties

musks

hundreds and thousands

rainbow balls

1 Cream butter and sugar until light and fluffy. Add eggs one at a time, beating well after each addition. Stir in the mashed banana, sour cream and oil.

2 Fold in flour and spice and pour mixture into 2 greased 20cm (8in) cake pans. Bake in moderate oven for 35 minutes or until cooked when tested. Set aside and cool completely.

3 To make the icing: Beat butter, sugar and milk together until creamy. Divide mixture in two, add yellow food colour to half and pink to the other half; add colouring drop by drop until desired intensity is achieved. The icing darkens slightly after an hour on cake. Cover icings with plastic wrap until ready to use.

4 Cut second cake as shown below and assemble.

5 Cover top and sides of cake 1 with the yellow icing, sprinkle top of cake with coconut. Carefully position the top of the clock (cake 2) against the top of cake 1, cover with pink icing.

6 Cover each mouse with pink icing and roll in hundreds and thousands. Make tail and whiskers out of licorice. If licorice is soft, it can be rolled out and cut. Cut numerals out of licorice. Decorate the rest of clock as desired.

Serves 12

Main picture: Banana Clock Cake
Above: Wheatmeal Faces

2 Dissolve jelly in hot water, add cold water. Refrigerate 30 minutes or until it begins to set. Do not allow jelly to set firm.

3 Arrange oranges skins on a tray, pour jelly into skins. Refrigerate until set.

4 Just before serving cut into quarters.

Makes 12

Cheese Muffins

½ cup cracked wheat

2½ cups self-raising flour

2 tblspn sugar

90g (3oz) grated cheese

60g (2oz) butter or margarine

6 spring onions (scallions), finely chopped

1 cup milk, approximately

1 egg, beaten

90g (3oz) grated cheese, extra

1 Cover cracked wheat in bowl with boiling water for 15 minutes, drain, rinse under water, drain well, dry between sheets of absorbent paper.

2 Sift flour and sugar into bowl, add cheese and cracked wheat.

3 Heat butter in pan, cook spring onions 5 minutes; stirring occasionally. Add ¾ cup milk, then egg, mix together. Add to flour mixture, stir lightly with fork.

4 Add more of remaining milk if necessary until mixture is a heavy dropping consistency.

5 Drop heaped teaspoonsful of mixture into deep, well greased muffin tins, sprinkle with extra cheese.

6 Bake in moderately hot oven 20 minutes or until golden brown. Serve hot with butter.

Makes 24

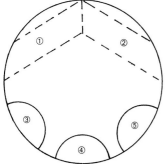

CUT OUT EACH SECTION AS SHOWN BY BROKEN LINES. REMAINDER OF CAKE IS NOT REQUIRED.
① & ② = PEAK ON CLOCK
③ ④ & ⑤ = MICE

Jelly Oranges

3 oranges

packet low-joule orange jelly

1½ cups hot water

½ cup cold water

1 Cut oranges in half, scoop out flesh without damaging the skins. The flesh is not used in this recipe.

BARCECUES

Fish and Pineapple Kebabs

1 red capsicum (pepper)

4 redfish fillets, cut into cubes

½ x 440g (14oz) can pineapple pieces, drained

1 green capsicum (pepper)

8 wooden skewers

½ tspn chopped mint

½ tblspn honey

½ tblspn oil

1 tblspn lemon juice

1 Cut capsicum into squares, about 2cm (¾in) wide, discard centre and seeds. Thread fish, pineapple and capsicum onto skewers alternately.

2 Brush with combined mint, honey, oil and lemon juice; barbecue until fish is cooked on both sides, basting frequently with marinade.

Makes 8 kebabs

Prawn (Shrimp) Kebabs with Butter Sauce

500g (1lb) green king prawns (shrimp)

1 large mango, chopped into large cubes

2 egg yolks

90g (3oz) butter, melted and bubbling

1 tblspn lemon juice

wooden skewers

1 Peel and devein prawns, leave tail intact. Thread 2 prawns onto each skewer, divided by a piece of mango.

2 Barbecue on each side until prawns change colour.

3 In a processor or blender, process egg yolks and lemon juice, pour bubbling butter into egg mixture while processor is running. Process 1 minute, or until sauce has thickened. Serve with kebabs.

Makes 6 kebabs

Lemon Lamb Chops

6 lamb loin chops

1 onion

2 tspn oregano leaves

½ cup olive oil

2 tblspn lemon juice

2 bay leaves

1 In a blender or processor, combine onion and oregano, mix until finely chopped. Add to oil and lemon juice and bay leaves, pour mixture over chops.

2 Barbecue one side, then turn and baste again with marinade and barbecue until cooked through.

Serves 6

Main picture: Prawn (Shrimp) Kebabs with Butter Sauce; Fish and Pineapple Kebabs Above: Lemon Lamb Chops

Falafel Patties

410g (6½oz) can chickpeas, drained

1 clove garlic, crushed

1 onion, chopped

1 green capsicum (pepper), chopped

½ tspn baking powder

¼ cup chopped parsley

1 tspn ground cumin

oil for barbecuing

1 Puree chickpeas in processor until smooth, add remaining ingredients and process to a smooth paste. Rest for 1 hour.

2 Shape mixture into flat patties. Rest 15 minutes. Cook patties on heated hot plate with a generous amount of oil until golden on both sides.

Serves 6

Steak and Zucchini (Courgette) Burgers

500g (1lb) minced steak

1 small onion, grated

3 small zucchini (courgettes), grated

1 tblspn soy sauce

1 tspn sesame oil

1 egg yolk

1 onion, sliced, extra

6 wholemeal buns

1 tomato, sliced

lettuce

1 Combine steak, onion, zucchini, soy sauce, sesame oil and egg yolk. Shape into six burgers.

2 Barbecue burgers and sliced onions on a lightly oiled hot plate until well cooked. Serve burger and onion on toasted buttered wholemeal buns with tomato and lettuce.

Serves 6

Basil Chicken Drumsticks

8 chicken drumsticks

30g (1oz) butter, softened

2 tblspn fresh chopped basil

2 tblspn chopped pine nuts

⅓ cup grated cheddar cheese

1 tblspn chopped parsley

1 In a large pan, add water, enough to cover drumsticks, bring to boil. Add drumsticks, and simmer for 10 minutes.

2 In a small bowl mix butter, basil, pine nuts, cheese and parsley until combined. Spread butter mixture between the skin and flesh of each drumstick.

3 Barbecue, brushing frequently with butter mixture until golden and cooked through.

Serves 4

Chicken Sausage Rolls

5 large pita bread

10 thick chicken sausages

125g (4oz) dried apricots

5 bacon rashers

toothpicks

2 carrots, grated

1 small lettuce, shredded

150g (5oz) alfalfa sprouts

2 cups grated cheddar cheese

1 Split each pita bread into 2 rounds.

2 Cut a slit in side of each sausage, place 2-3 apricots in each one, wrap in half a bacon rasher, secure with toothpick. Barbecue until cooked.

3 Place a hot sausage with toothpick removed on each pita round. Sprinkle with grated carrot, shredded lettuce, sprouts and cheese. Roll up pita bread.

Serves 10

Honey Pork Fillets

6 pork fillets

¼ cup tomato sauce

¼ cup honey

2 tspn soy sauce

1 Combine fillets with tomato sauce, honey and soy sauce, stand one hour, turning occasionally.

2 Barbecue over low heat until cooked through, brushing occasionally with remaining marinade.

Serves 6

Vegetable Foil Parcels

2 bacon rashers, chopped
3 cups cooked brown rice
2 tblspn chopped parsley
3 carrots, chopped
18 baby green squash
6 small pieces broccoli
30g (1oz) butter
½ cup chopped chives
1 cup grated cheddar cheese

1 Cut 6 pieces of foil about 24cm x 30cm (9½ x 12in). Cook bacon in pan until crisp, drain on absorbent paper.

2 Combine bacon, rice and parsley in bowl. Divide evenly between centre of foil pieces.

3 Boil, steam or microwave vegetables until half cooked, drain. Divide vegetables evenly on top of rice mixture. Dot with butter, sprinkle with combined chives and cheese.

4 Wrap parcels tightly, barbecue until vegetables are tender.

Serves 6

Fruit Kebabs

1 small pineapple
2 kiwifruits
1 punnet large strawberries
8 wooden skewers

DRESSING

1 tblspn lemon juice
2 tblspn orange juice
1 tblspn honey
1 tblspn orange rind, grated

1 Peel and core pineapple, cut into 2½cm (1in) cubes. Peel and quarter kiwifruit, remove stem from strawberries. Thread fruit alternately onto skewers.

2 Make orange dressing: combine all ingredients in small bowl, beat well. Brush skewers with orange dressing; barbecue, turning frequently. Baste with dressing while cooking.

Makes about 12

Above: Basil Chicken Drumsticks. Below: Fruit Kebabs

Chicken Honey Rolls with Curry Seasoning

8 chicken thigh fillets

¼ cup cracked wheat

15g (½oz) butter

1 onion, chopped

2 tblspn sultanas

1 tspn curry powder

4 spinach leaves, chopped finely

HONEY GLAZE

2 tblspn honey

1 tspn curry powder

1 tspn light soy sauce

1 tspn melted butter

1 Pour boiling water over cracked wheat and soak for 30 minutes, drain.

2 Melt butter in pan, add onion and sultanas, cook for 3 minutes. Add curry, cracked wheat and spinach, stir over heat until spinach is tender.

3 Place chicken thighs skin side down, spread top with spinach mixture, roll up, secure with a skewer. Place rolls on a greased baking tray.

4 Combine all honey glaze ingredients in a small saucepan. Stir over low heat until honey has melted, about 2 minutes. Brush each chicken roll with the glaze. Bake in moderate oven for 30 minutes, basting regularly with glaze.

Serves 4

Baked Snapper with Pineapple Seasoning

1 whole snapper

2 tblspn cracked wheat

450g (14oz) tin unsweetened pineapple pieces

2 spring onions (scallions), chopped

½ red capsicum (pepper), chopped

1 tblspn wheatgerm

1 egg

½ cup chicken stock

1 tblspn cornflour

1 tspn light soy sauce

½ cup reserved pineapple juice

oil, for brushing fish

1 Soak cracked wheat in boiling water for 20 minutes; strain; drain well.

2 Wash fish under cold water.

3 In a medium bowl, combine wheat, half the pineapple pieces (drain and reserve ½ cup pineapple juice) half the spring onions, half the capsicum, wheatgerm and egg; mix well.

4 Fill the cavity of fish with the pineapple seasoning mixture. Place fish on a greased oven tray, brush with oil and bake in a moderate oven for 30 minutes.

5 In a small saucepan, combine chicken stock, cornflour, soy sauce and pineapple juice. Stir sauce over a low heat until mixture boils and thickens, add remaining pineapple pieces, spring onions and capsicum, serve over fish.

Serves 4

Chicken Honey Rolls with Curry Seasoning; Baked Snapper with Pineapple Seasoning

Spiral Pasta Salad

1 cup spiral pasta

1 medium red capsicum (pepper), chopped

1 medium green capsicum (pepper), chopped

125g (4oz) lean leg ham, chopped

2 tblspn chopped fresh chives

2 tblspn white vinegar

½ tspn sugar

1 tspn curry powder

2 tblspn oil

1 Cook pasta in boiling water 10 minutes or until just tender. Drain, rinse well under cold running water until cold, drain well.

2 Place pasta in large bowl with capsicums, ham and chives.

3 Combine remaining ingredients in a jar, shake well, pour over salad, toss well.

Serves 4

Watermelon with Passionfruit Yoghurt

¼ small watermelon

200g (6½oz) carton low fat natural yoghurt

1 passionfruit

2 tspn honey

1 Cut watermelon flesh into 2cm (¾in) cubes.

2 Combine yoghurt with passionfruit pulp and honey.

3 Serve melon in bowls, spoon passionfruit yoghurt over top.

Serves 4

Above: Strawberry and Mango Salad with Honey Cream. Right: Pea and Mushroom Flan

Strawberry and Mango Salad with Honey Cream

| 1 punnet strawberries |
| 2 mangoes |
| 1 tblspn honey |
| ½ cup sour cream |

1 Slice strawberries and mango flesh into 2cm (¾in) cubes. Arrange decoratively in 4 dishes.

2 Combine honey and sour cream, mix well. Spoon cream mixture over fruit. Chill before serving.

Serves 4

Pea and Mushroom Flan

FLAN PASTRY

| 1½ cups wholemeal plain flour |
| 2 tblspn finely grated Parmesan cheese |
| 125g (4oz) butter, chopped |
| 2 tblspn milk, approximately |

FILLING

| 2 cups cooked peas |
| 100g (3½oz) baby mushrooms, sliced |
| ½ cup cream |
| ½ cup cottage cheese |
| 1 cup grated cheddar cheese |
| 2 eggs |

1 Combine flour and cheese in a bowl, rub in butter. Add enough milk to mix to a firm dough.

2 Knead lightly on a floured surface, wrap dough, refrigerate for 30 minutes.

3 Re-roll pastry to fit a 23cm (9in) flan tin. Cover pastry with grease proof paper, and sprinkle with pastry weights. Cook in a hot oven for 10 minutes. Remove paper and weights and cook for a further 5 minutes.

4 Spread peas and mushrooms evenly into flan. In a medium bowl combine cream, cottage cheese, ½ of the cheese and eggs, mix well. Pour over peas.

5 Sprinkle the remaining cheese over top and bake in moderate oven 30-35 minutes.

Serves 6

Indonesian Salad

4 cups shredded cabbage

250g (½lb) green beans, sliced

1 carrot, cut into strips

250g (½lb) small new potatoes, halved

1 cucumber, cut into strips

4 hard-boiled eggs

DRESSING

1 tblspn oil

1 onion, finely chopped

1 clove garlic, crushed

1 tspn ground cumin

1 tspn curry powder

½ tspn ground coriander

1 tblspn white vinegar

1 tblspn sugar

½ cup crunchy peanut butter

2 tblspn fruit chutney

1½ cups water

1 Bring a large saucepan of water to the boil, add cabbage, cook 1 minute, remove with tongs, and drain. Add beans and carrots, cook for 2 minutes, remove with tongs, drain well. Add potatoes to water, boil until tender.

2 Put all vegetables on platter with halved eggs, refrigerate until ready to serve with dressing.

3 To make dressing, heat oil in a medium saucepan, add onion and garlic, cook 2 minutes. Add remaining ingredients and simmer for 15 minutes, stirring occasionally. Cool to room temperature, serve with vegetables.

Serves 4

Indonesian Salad

Easy Bean Salad

310g (10oz) can red kidney beans

310g (10oz) can butter (cannelloni) beans

310g (10oz) can four bean mix

1 stick celery, sliced

1 Lebanese cucumber, sliced

2 spring onions (scallions), chopped

¼ cup French dressing

2 tblspn chopped fresh parsley

1 tspn French mustard

1 Drain beans, rinse under cold running water; drain well.

2 Combine beans, celery, cucumber and spring onions in bowl.

3 Pour over combined dressing, parsley and mustard; mix gently until well combined.

Serves 6

Baked Beans with Sausages

2 x 440g (14oz) cans baked beans in tomato sauce

1 stick celery, chopped

125g (4oz) baby mushrooms, wiped

1 green capsicum (pepper), chopped

450g (14oz) pineapple pieces, drained

1 tspn Worcestershire sauce

200g (6½oz) pure chicken sausages

1 Combine beans, celery, mushrooms, capsicum and pineapple pieces in ovenproof dish. Stir in Worcestershire sauce.

2 Grill sausages until golden on all sides, chop into 1cm (½in) pieces. Add to bean mixture.

3 Bake uncovered in moderate oven 30 minutes. Serve with warm wholemeal bread.

Serves 6

Cheesy Oatburgers

1 cup grated cheddar cheese

¼ cup green capsicum (pepper), chopped finely

1 tomato, chopped finely

1 small onion, chopped finely

1 cup oats

2 eggs, lightly beaten

⅓ cup plain flour

oil for frying

1 In a medium bowl combine cheese, capsicum, tomato, onion, oats, egg and flour; mix well. Divide mixture into six smaller portions and shape into patties.

2 Heat oil in a large frying pan, add oatburgers and using a spatula, turn over and cook other side. Cook 3 minutes each side, or until oatburgers are golden.

3 Serve on a wholemeal roll with salad.

Makes 6

Easy Wholemeal Muffins

90g (3oz) butter

½ cup honey

1 tspn grated lemon rind

2 eggs

1½ cups wholemeal plain flour

1½ tspn baking powder

1 tspn cinnamon

1 cup sultanas

1 Turn oven on to moderately hot, 190°C (375°F).

2 Beat butter, honey and lemon rind in small bowl with electric mixer until combined.

3 Add eggs, beat until well combined.

4 Sift flour, baking powder and cinnamon into a bowl, return husks from sifter.

5 Stir flour mixture into butter mixture, then add sultanas, mix well.

6 Grease 18 patty tins. Fill patty tins just over half full. Bake 20 minutes. Serve hot with butter.

Makes 18

Muesli Bars

60g (2oz) butter

½ cup brown sugar

2 eggs

¾ cup plain flour

½ tspn baking powder

1 cup Swiss style muesli

2 tspn grated lemon rind

2 tblspn lemon juice

½ cup sultanas

½ cup chopped dried apricots

1 Turn oven onto moderate, 180°C (350°F).

2 Beat butter, brown sugar and eggs in small bowl with electric mixer until smooth.

3 Sift flour and baking powder together, add to mixer, beat well.

4 Stir in muesli, lemon rind and juice, sultanas and apricots.

5 Spread into prepared tin. Bake for 30 minutes.

6 Cool on wire rack. Cut into squares.

Makes 16

Cheesy Oatburgers

Left: Apple Slice. Above: Oven Fried Chicken

Apple Slice

100g (3½oz) butter

½ cup brown sugar

2 eggs

½ cup self-raising flour

½ cup wholemeal self-raising flour

1 cup cornflour

3 cooking apples, peeled

4 tblspn caster sugar

icing sugar for decoration

1 Beat together butter, brown sugar and eggs until light and creamy. Sift in flours and cornflour; mix well.

2 Spread half the batter evenly over the base of a greased 30cm x 20cm (12 x 8in) lamington tin.

3 Grate the apples and add to the remaining half of flour mixture. Sprinkle base layer with caster sugar, then spread apple mixture evenly over top.

4 Bake in moderate oven 25-30 minutes. Cool, dust with icing sugar. Cut into squares, serve with whipped cream if desired.

Serves 12

Oven Fried Chicken

6 chicken drumsticks

½ cup natural yoghurt

1 tblspn lemon juice

1 tspn Worcestershire sauce

¼ tspn paprika

1 clove garlic, crushed

1 cup packaged dry breadcrumbs

1 Mix yoghurt, lemon juice, Worcestershire sauce, paprika and garlic in a bowl. Coat each drumstick in yoghurt mixture, roll in breadcrumbs.

2 Place drumsticks in a greased baking dish. Bake in a moderate oven for 45 minutes or until cooked.

Makes 6

Oven Potatoes

4 medium potatoes, peeled, washed and sliced

1 onion, finely chopped

30g (1oz) butter

1 cup milk

½ cup grated cheese

1 Turn oven on to moderate, 180°C (350°F).

2 Grease a casserole dish with butter.

3 Arrange potatoes in casserole dish. Sprinkle onion over. Dot with butter.

4 Pour milk over potatoes, sprinkle with cheese.

5 Bake, uncovered for 1½ hours.

Serves 4

Fish in Foil

4 fish fillets

2 tblspn mild mustard

1 tspn grated lemon rind

30g (1oz) butter

⅓ cup cream

1 carrot, grated

½ cup grated cheese

1 Turn oven onto moderate, 180°C (350°F). Tear off four large pieces of foil. Place fish fillet on each piece. Spread a little mustard on each one.

2 Put a little lemon rind on each fillet. Dot each one with butter. Place a tablespoon of cream on each one.

3 Sprinkle with grated carrot and cheese.

4 Seal foil securely, place onto oven tray. Bake for 30 minutes.

5 Serve in the foil.

Serves 4

Tomato Salad

6 ripe tomatoes

1 tblspn chopped basil

1 tblspn vinegar

¼ cup finely chopped parsley

DRESSING

¼ cup French dressing

¼ cup soy mayonnaise

1 Wash tomatoes, slice evenly and thinly. Arrange tomatoes decoratively on plate.

2 Combine basil and vinegar and pour over tomatoes. Sprinkle parsley over the top.

3 Combine French dressing and mayonnaise in a jug; mix well. Pour dressing over tomatoes.

Serves 4

Asparagus Omelette

2 eggs

1 tblspn water

1 tspn butter

½ x 340g (11oz) can asparagus, drained

1 Warm omelette pan over a very low heat.

2 Lightly mix eggs and water. Brush pan with butter, turn up heat. Pour the egg mixture into pan, tipping pan as you pour.

3 As uncooked egg runs to the edge, drag cooked eggs to centre. Cook until the top of egg mixture is set.

4 Place 2-3 asparagus spears across centre of omelette, flip outside edges into centre, one over the other, covering asparagus. Using spatula turn onto serving plate, serve immediately.

Serves 1

Toasted Cheese Snack

6 slices brown bread

2 tspn mild mustard

6 slices pressed chicken

1 cup grated cheese

3 tblspn mayonnaise

2 spring onions (scallions), chopped

1 Toast bread. Spread each slice of toast with a little mustard.

2 Put a slice of pressed chicken on each slice of toast.

3 Combine cheese, mayonnaise and spring onion in bowl, mix well. Spread cheese mixture on top of each chicken slice.

4 Line griller with foil. Place snacks under a hot griller until bubbling, about 3 minutes.

5 Use oven gloves to remove from griller, serve on plates and remember to turn griller off.

Serves 4-6

Tomato Salad; Asparagus Omelette

117

DESSERTS AND SWEET TREATS

Sugar and spice and all things nice — that's how the old nursery rhyme goes. Here are recipes to satisfy the demand for "puddings" in a variety of ways that will leave you feeling good too.

Wholemeal Banana Pancakes with Strawberry Sauce

1 cup wholemeal plain flour

1¼ cups skim milk

1 egg

2 tspn honey

1 tspn oil

2 tblspn chopped raisins

1 tblspn water

2 tblspn honey

1 tspn lemon juice

2 bananas sliced

250g (½lb) punnet strawberries

2 tspn lemon juice, extra

1 Sift flour into bowl, gradually stir in combined milk, egg and honey, beat until smooth, stir in oil; stand for 30 minutes.

2 Heat small pan, grease lightly. Pour about ¼ cup batter into pan, cook until browned underneath, turn, cook other side. Repeat with remaining batter.

3 Soak raisins in water 15 minutes, add honey, lemon rind, lemon juice, pour over bananas.

4 Spoon small amount of banana mixture onto each crepe and fold. Place in single layer in oven proof dish, cover, bake in moderate oven 10 minutes or until heated through.

5 Process strawberries and lemon juice until smooth. Serve banana pancakes with strawberry sauce.

Serves 6

Banana Whip

1 large banana, mashed

2 egg whites

2 tblspn sugar

2 tblspn lemon juice

1 tspn cocoa

1 Beat egg whites until firm peaks form.

2 Fold in sugar, mashed banana, lemon juice and cocoa.

3 Pour into dessert dishes. Serve immediately.

Serves 4

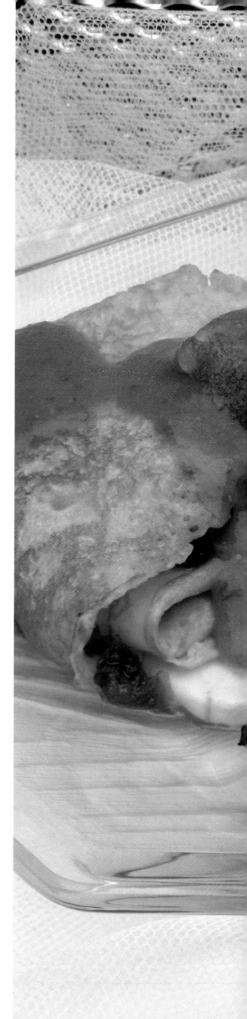

Wholemeal Banana Pancakes with Strawberry Sauce

Baked Apples

4 apples

½ cup sultanas

2 tblspn chopped pecan nuts

1 cup orange juice

½ cup brown sugar

30g (1oz) butter

1 tspn cinnamon

1 Remove most of core from each apple, leave base of apples intact, fill each cavity with combined sultanas and pecans.

2 Slit skin around the centre of each apple to prevent apples bursting during cooking. Place apples in ovenproof dish.

3 Combine orange juice, sugar, butter and cinnamon in pan, stir over heat until sugar is dissolved, bring to boil, boil 3 minutes without stirring. Pour sauce over apples.

4 Bake in moderate oven 40 minutes or until apples are tender. Baste apples occasionally with sauce during cooking.

Serves 4

Rockmelon Mousse

5 cups chopped rockmelon

¼ cup honey

200g (6½oz) carton low fat plain yoghurt

1 tblspn gelatine

2 tblspn water

1 Blend or process rockmelon, honey and yoghurt until smooth.

2 Sprinkle gelatine over water, dissolve over hot water (or microwave on high for about 20 seconds).

3 Stir gelatine mixture into melon mixture. Pour mixture into 4 serving dishes, refrigerate several hours or until set.

Serves 4

Raspberry and Yoghurt Jellies

9g (¼oz) sachet low-joule raspberry jelly

100g (3½oz) frozen raspberries

200g (6½oz) carton low fat raspberry yoghurt

1 Make jelly according to instructions on packet, allow to cool slightly.

2 Add raspberries and yoghurt, mix well.

3 Pour into 4 individual serving dishes. Refrigerate until set.

Serves 4

Rockmelon Mousse

Pears and Green Grapes

4 ripe pears, peeled, halved, cored

175g (5½oz) cream cheese, room temperature

¼ cup caster sugar

1 tspn grated lemon rind

350g (11oz) green seedless grapes, halved

1 Combine cream cheese, sugar and lemon rind.

2 Arrange pear halves cut side down on serving plates. Coat with cream cheese mixture.

3 Press grape halves onto pears to cover them. Refrigerate until ready to serve.

Serves 4

Apricot Yoghurt Freeze

1 cup apricot jam

1 cup low fat plain yoghurt

1 cup instant skim milk powder

2 egg whites, stiffly beaten

1 Place jam, yoghurt and skim milk powder into a processor or blender, process for 1 minute.

2 Transfer mixture to a large bowl and gently fold in egg whites. Pour mixture into 20 x 10cm (8 x 4in) loaf tin and freeze.

Serves 4

Wholemeal Pumpkin Pie

1 sheet wholemeal shortcrust pastry

750g (1½lb) pumpkin

¼ tspn each cinnamon, cloves, nutmeg and ginger

2 eggs, separated

¾ cup cream

¾ cup milk

¾ cup honey

1 Line a 23cm (9in) pie plate with pastry. Trim and decorate edges.

2 Peel pumpkin, remove seeds, cut into pieces; cook in boiling salted water until tender, drain well.

3 Blend pumpkin in processor or blender with remaining ingredients.

4 Pour filling into pie plate. Bake in hot oven 15 minutes, reduce heat to moderate, bake further 45 minutes or until set.

Serves 4-6

Wholemeal Bread and Butter Pudding

4 slices wholegrain bread

butter

2 tblspn sultanas

4 eggs

¼ cup sugar

2 cups milk

1 tspn vanilla

nutmeg or cinnamon

1 Trim crusts from bread, butter each slice. Cut each slice diagonally into four triangles.

2 Sprinkle sultanas into ovenproof dish. Neatly arrange bread, buttered side up, over sultanas.

3 Lightly beat eggs, sugar, milk and vanilla together, pour over bread, stand 10 minutes.

4 Sprinkle lightly with nutmeg or cinnamon. Bake in moderate oven 40 minutes or until golden brown.

Serves 4

Pears and Green Grapes; Apricot Yoghurt Freeze

Above: Vanilla Ice-Cream; Right: Apple Crunch; Fruit Salad with Strawberry Yoghurt

Vanilla Ice-cream

Great for ice-cream cones.

⅓ cup caster sugar

⅓ cup water

1 tspn gelatine

⅔ cup skim milk powder

2 cups skim milk

1 tspn white vinegar

2 tspn vanilla essence

1 Combine sugar and water in small saucepan, add gelatine, stir constantly over heat without boiling until sugar and gelatine are dissolved.

2 Transfer mixture to bowl, whisk in milk powder, then gradually beat in skim milk with electric mixer.

3 Pour into 2 lamington tins; cover with foil, freeze for about 1 hour or until almost set.

4 Transfer mixture to large bowl, add vinegar and essence, beat with electric mixer until thick and creamy. Return to lamington tins, cover, freeze for about 3 hours or overnight.

Makes about 1½ litres (6 cups)

Apple Crunch

6 Granny Smith apples, peeled, cored, sliced

½ cup honey

1 cup wholemeal plain flour

1 cup rolled oats

¼ cup wheatgerm

¼ cup raw sugar

125g (4oz) butter, chopped

1 Arrange apple slices over base of a shallow ovenproof dish. Drizzle honey evenly over apples.

2 Combine flour, oats, wheatgerm and sugar in a bowl. Rub in butter until mixture resembles fine breadcrumbs.

3 Spoon mixture over apples. Bake in moderately hot oven 1 hour or until golden brown.

Serves 6

Fruit Salad with Strawberry Yoghurt

250g (½lb) punnet strawberries

2 medium Kiwi fruit, sliced

1 mango, sliced

2 peaches, sliced

¾ cup low fat natural yoghurt

2 tblspn strawberry jam

1 Divide fruit into 4 serving dishes.

2 Combine yoghurt and jam and pour over fruit.

Serves 4

Baked Brown Rice Custard

¼ cup brown short grain rice

3 eggs

⅓ cup sugar

1 tspn vanilla

¼ cup sultanas

2½ cups milk

nutmeg or cinnamon

1 Cook rice in pan of boiling water 20 minutes, drain well.

2 Beat eggs, sugar and vanilla together, add rice and sultanas, gradually whisk in milk.

3 Pour into ovenproof dish, stand in baking dish with enough hot water to come halfway up sides of dish.

4 Sprinkle lightly with nutmeg or cinnamon. Bake in moderate oven 45 minutes, or until set and lightly browned.

Serves 4

Apple Snow

3 Granny Smith apples, sliced

1 cup sultanas

⅓ cup honey

pinch cinnamon

2 tblspn slivered almonds

1 tblspn lemon juice

2 egg whites

2 tblspn sugar

1 Arrange sliced apple over base of shallow ovenproof dish.

2 Sprinkle with sultanas and drizzle with honey. Sprinkle with cinnamon. Bake in moderate oven 10 minutes.

3 Toast almonds on oven tray in moderate oven 5 minutes. Sprinkle lemon juice over apples.

4 Beat egg whites until firm peaks form, fold in sugar and almonds. Spread over apples and bake in hot oven until lightly browned, about 3-5 minutes.

Serves 4

Jelly and Custard

9g (2 tspn) sachet low-joule jelly

425g (13½oz) can cherries, drained, stoned

375ml (12 fl. oz) can evaporated skim milk

1 egg, lightly beaten

⅓ cup caster sugar

1 tblspn plain flour

¼ cup water

2 tspn vanilla essence

1 Make jelly according to instructions on packet, pour into lamington tin, cool, refrigerate until set.

2 Chop jelly roughly, spoon into 4 individual serving dishes, top with cherries. Refrigerate while making custard.

3 Combine milk, egg, sugar and combined flour and water in a saucepan, stir constantly over heat until mixture boils and thickens.

4 Stir in essence, cover surface of custard with plastic wrap to prevent skin forming, cool to room temperature.

5 Spoon custard over jelly and cherries; refrigerate until ready to serve.

Serves 4

Jelly and Custard

126

TEMPERATURE AND MEASUREMENT EQUIVALENTS

OVEN TEMPERATURES

	Fahrenheit	Celsius
Very slow	250°	120°
Slow	275–300°	140–150°
Moderately slow	325°	160°
Moderate	350°	180°
Moderately hot	375°	190°
Hot	400–450°	200–230°
Very hot	475–500°	250–260°

CUP AND SPOON MEASURES

Measures given in our recipes refer to the standard metric cup and spoon sets approved by the Standards Association of Australia.

A basic metric cup set consists of 1 cup, ½ cup, ⅓ cup and ¼ cup sizes.

The basic spoon set comprises 1 tablespoon, 1 teaspoon, ½ teaspoon and ¼ teaspoon. These sets are available at leading department, kitchen and hardware stores.

IMPERIAL/METRIC CONVERSION CHART

MASS (WEIGHT)
(Approximate conversions for cookery purposes.)

Imperial	Metric	Imperial	Metric
½ oz	15 g	10 oz	315 g
1 oz	30 g	11 oz	345 g
2 oz	60 g	12 oz (¾ lb)	375 g
3 oz	90 g	13 oz	410 g
4 oz (¼ lb)	125 g	14 oz	440 g
5 oz	155 g	15 oz	470 g
6 oz	185 g	16 oz (1 lb)	500 g (0.5 kg)
7 oz	220 g	24 oz (1½ lb)	750 g
8 oz (½ lb)	250 g	32 oz (2 lb)	1000 g (1 kg)
9 oz	280 g	3 lb	1500 g (1.5 kg)

METRIC CUP AND SPOON SIZES

Cup	Spoon
¼ cup = 60 ml	¼ teaspoon = 1.25 ml
⅓ cup = 80 ml	½ teaspoon = 2.5 ml
½ cup = 125 ml	1 teaspoon = 5 ml
1 cup = 250 ml	1 tablespoon = 20 ml

LIQUIDS

Imperial	Cup*	Metric
1 fl oz		30 ml
2 fl oz	¼ cup	60 ml
3 fl oz		100 ml
4 fl oz	½ cup	125 ml

LIQUIDS (cont'd)

Imperial	Cup*	Metric
5 fl oz (¼ pint)		150 ml
6 fl oz	¾ cup	200 ml
8 fl oz	1 cup	250 ml
10 fl oz (½ pint)	1¼ cups	300 ml
12 fl oz	1½ cups	375 ml
14 fl oz	1¾ cups	425 ml
15 fl oz		475 ml
16 fl oz	2 cups	500 ml
20 fl oz (1 pint)	2½ cups	600 ml

* Cup measures are the same in Imperial and Metric.

LENGTH

Inches	Centimetres	Inches	Centimetres
¼	0.5	7	18
½	1	8	20
¾	2	9	23
1	2.5	10	25
1½	4	12	30
2	5	14	35
2½	6	16	40
3	8	18	45
4	10	20	50
6	15		

NB: 1 cm = 10 mm.